THE SCHOOL MATHEMATICS PROJECT

When the S.M.P. was founded in 1961, its objective was to devise radically new mathematics courses, with accompanying G.C.E. syllabuses and examinations, which would reflect, more adequately than did the traditional syllabuses, the up-to-date nature and usages of mathematics.

The first stage of this objective is now more or less complete. *Books 1–5* form the main series of pupils' texts, starting at the age of 11 + and leading to the O-level examination in 'S.M.P. Mathematics', while *Books 3T, 4* and *5* give a three-year course to the same O-level examination. (*Books T* and *T4*, together with their Supplement, represent the first attempt at this three-year course, but they may be regarded as obsolete.) *Advanced Mathematics Books 1–4* cover the syllabus for the A-level examination in 'S.M.P. Mathematics' and in preparation are five (or more) shorter texts covering the material of various sections of the A-level examination in 'S.M.P. Further Mathematics'. There are two books for 'S.M.P. Additional Mathematics' at O-level. Every book is accompanied by a Teacher's Guide.

For the convenience of schools, the S.M.P. has an arrangement whereby its examinations are made available by every G.C.E. Examining Board, and it is most grateful to the Secretaries of the eight Boards for their cooperation in this. At the same time, most Boards now offer their own syllabuses in 'modern mathematics' for which the S.M.P. texts are suitable.

By 1967, it had become clear from experience in comprehensive schools that the mathematical content of the S.M.P. texts was suitable for a much wider range of pupil than had been originally anticipated, but that the presentation needed adaptation. Thus it was decided to produce a new series, *Books A–H*, which could serve as a secondary school course starting at the age of 11 +. These books are specially suitable for pupils aiming at a C.S.E. examination; however, the framework of the C.S.E. examinations is such that it is inappropriate for the S.M.P. to offer its own examination as it does for the G.C.E.

The completion of all these books does not mean that the S.M.P. has no more to offer to the cause of curriculum research. The team of S.M.P. writers, now numbering some thirty school and university mathematicians, is continually testing and revising old work and preparing for new. At the same time, the effectiveness of the S.M.P.'s work depends, as it always has done, on obtaining reactions from active teachers—and also from pupils—in the classroom. Readers of the texts can therefore send their comments to the S.M.P. in the knowledge that they will be warmly welcomed.

Finally, the year-by-year activity of the S.M.P. is recorded in the annual Director's Reports which readers are encouraged to obtain on request to the S.M.P. Office at Westfield College, University of London, Kidderpore Avenue, London NW3 7ST.

THE SCHOOL MATHEMATICS PROJECT

BOOK A

[METRIC]

CAMBRIDGE
AT THE UNIVERSITY PRESS

1970

Published by the Syndics of the Cambridge University Press
Bentley House, 200 Euston Road, London NW1 2DB
American Branch: 32 East 57th Street, New York, N.Y.10022

© Cambridge University Press 1968

Metric edition © Cambridge University Press 1970

Library of Congress Catalogue Card Number: 68–21399

ISBNs: 0 521 07879 2 limp bound
       0 521 08356 7 cased edition

First published 1968
Reprinted 1969 (twice)
Metricated 1970
Reprinted 1971 1972

Printed in Great Britain
at the University Printing House, Cambridge
(Brooke Crutchley, University Printer)

Preface

This is the first of eight books designed to cover a course suitable for those who wish to take a CSE Examination on one of the reformed mathematics syllabuses.

The material is based upon the first four books of the O-level series, SMP Books 1–4. The connection is maintained to the extent that it will be possible to change from one series to the other at the end of the first year, or even at a later stage. For example, having started with Books A and B, a pupil will be able to move to Book 2.

Within each year's work, the material has been entirely broken down and rewritten. The differences between the two series fall under five headings:

(i) The emphasis placed upon preliminary investigation and question in the O-level books has been taken up and developed in this series. From the Prelude, which is entirely experimental, through to the chapter on polyhedra, which involves a very great deal of practical work, each chapter involves activity and investigation as well as establishing the main points by a process of question and answer.

(ii) The O-level books have tended to assume rather more knowledge of some subjects than has been found entirely justified for the average pupil. In this new series, more time is given to the earlier stages and some sections on preliminary work have been added.

(iii) The original chapters have been divided into several parts for two reasons: first, to allow pupils more time to absorb one point before moving on to its development; secondly, by providing a smaller interval between one discussion of a subject and the next, to reduce the need for extensive revision.

(iv) Preludes and Interludes have been added. In general, the Preludes will be an integral part of the book. Later chapters will often depend upon, and sometimes specifically refer to, the experiences gained from them. The Interludes will tend to be separate from the main development of the text. In general, they will describe situations from which mathematics can be drawn. Most of these situations will be internal to the classroom, as in the designing of patterns described in Book A; but some, such as the surveying in Book C, will involve work outside the classroom. In all cases, pupils should be encouraged to formulate their own questions, and so to realize contexts within which mathematics is developed.

(v) There have been some small changes in mathematical content taken from Book 1 and similar small changes may be expected in later books. For example, there is no chapter on Sets. The subject and the notation have been introduced where necessary in Book A, but the study of Venn diagrams and of their attendant problems has been postponed to a later book. Some statistics and topology have been brought into Book B; also a consideration of non-numerical relations. These three subjects, all fundamental to the course, are started in Book 2, but they are interesting and suitable for Book B.

The main differences between the content of these two SMP series and that of the more traditional texts arise from two convictions: first, that understanding and interest in the general statements of mathematics stem from experience of a wide range of particular situations and from confidence that questions of mathematical significance can be asked and answered in many of these situations; secondly, that these experiences should arise inside as well as outside mathematics. Thus, it is useful to have discussed and manipulated expressions in symbols concerned with sets, transformations and matrices in order to obtain a deeper understanding of the significance of these symbols, before perfecting the techniques of equation-solving within the field of real numbers. It is worth discovering a wide variety of relations and of methods for illustrating them, before applying this knowledge to a discussion of mathematical functions, equations and graphs. It is useful to gain considerable experience of shapes and of methods of measuring and describing them by studying polyhedra and by considering transformations of figures in the plane, before developing any formal body of geometrical theorems.

For these reasons, the newer topics should be considered to be an integral part of the course, not something to be learnt at the side of, and separate from it.

In this book, Book A, two chapters are devoted to consideration of the patterns among the counting numbers; these lead to sections on various sequences of numbers as well as on factors and multiples. Two short chapters are included to remind pupils of the basic ideas, but not the manipulative techniques, of fractions; a chapter on number bases emphasizes the importance of position in the numeral system, and this prepares for the chapter on decimals. The chapter on coordinates lays a foundation for later work on graphs. The several geometry chapters—on angle, symmetry, polygons and polyhedra—are all designed to give experience of shape and methods of describing it, though the problems of measurement of length have been delayed to Book B.

Answers to exercises are not printed at the end of this book but are contained in the companion Teacher's Guide which gives a detailed commentary on the pupil's text. In this series, the answers and commentary are interleaved with the main texts.

Contents

Contents

Acknowledgements

The principal authors, on whose contributions the S.M.P. texts are largely based, are named in the annual Reports. Many other authors have also provided original material, and still more have been directly involved in the revision of draft versions of chapters and books. The Project gratefully acknowledges the contributions which they and their schools have made.

This book—*Book A*—has been written by

Catherine Braithwaite	W. Mrozowski
D. Dorrian	Margaret Wilkinson
Joyce Harris	E. Williamson
K. Lewis	

and edited by P. G. Bowie assisted by Elizabeth Evans.

The Project is most grateful for the advice on points of fundamental mathematics given by Dr. J. V. Armitage.

The drawings at the chapter openings in this book are by Penny Wager.

The Project is grateful to the BBC for permission to use the photograph of Harry Worth and the sketch of a dalek.

We are much indebted to the Cambridge University Press for their cooperation and help at all times in the preparation of this book.

The Project owes a great deal to its secretary, Miss A. J. Freeman; also to Mrs E. L. Humphreys and Mrs E. Muir for their assistance and for their typing in connection with this book.

Prelude

1. THE THREE BY THREE PINBOARD

Let us see how much mathematics we can find in a simple situation. We shall need a piece of wood with nine small nails hammered into it to form the above square pattern. Use elastic bands to carry out the following experiments:

Experiment 1

How many squares can you make?
Use spotty paper or squared paper to record each separate discovery, and then show all your results on one diagram.

Experiment 2

How many rectangles can you make? Record your results.

You probably found these two experiments fairly easy. It is possible to make only six squares and four other rectangles. When we think about other shapes, such as triangles, the task of finding all of them is more difficult. We shall split this task into parts.

1

Experiment 3

Find triangles which have two sides equal in length like these:

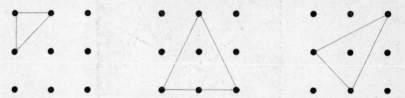

These are called *isosceles* triangles.
Record your results carefully. There are many triangles to be found.

Experiment 4

Find triangles which do not have any equal sides but which do have a square corner, such as:

Experiment 5

Are there any other triangles?
How many triangles can you find altogether?
Can you find a triangle with all three sides the same length?

Experiment 6

These shapes are called *parallelograms*. How many can you find that have no square corners?

Experiment 7

Shapes which have four straight sides are called *quadrilaterals*. Apart from squares, rectangles and parallelograms without square corners, what other quadrilaterals can you make?

Experiment 8

Can you make shapes which have five, six or seven sides? Is it possible to make a shape with eight straight sides?

Experiment 9

Start •   •   •

•   •   •

•   •   • Finish

What is the shortest route from the top left corner to the bottom right? What is the longest route you can find? How many routes do you think there are? (You may use each nail only once and the bands should not cross over.)

2. THE FIVE BY FIVE PINBOARD

If, instead of nine nails, twenty-five are used, a five by five pinboard can be made. Finding all the squares, all the triangles, and so on, is now more difficult than it was with a three by three board. However, there are some easier problems which we can consider.

Experiment 10

Using one elastic band as a boundary, the board can be halved
       in this way,   or even this.

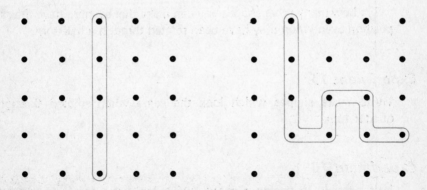

In how many different ways can you halve the board?

Experiment 11

In how many different ways can you quarter the board?

Experiment 12

How many different sizes of square can you make?

Experiment 13

See who can make a shape with the greatest number of sides.

Experiment 14

Make this shape on your pinboard. If somebody came along while you were not looking and turned the board through half of a complete turn, would you know what had happened?

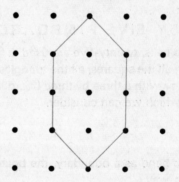

See how many other shapes you can make that seem to have the same position even when they have been rotated through a half-turn.

Experiment 15

Try to make shapes which look the same when rotated through a quarter-turn.

Experiment 16

Is it possible to design a shape which looks the same when rotated through an eighth of a turn?

Experiment 17

Somebody was in a hurry and left this shape on his board saying that the other half was the same anyway.

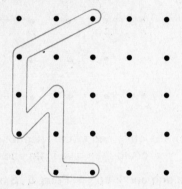

Can you complete the shape? Is there more than one possible answer?

Experiment 18

Design other shapes which could have been given for Experiment 17. Work with a partner. Make your half and ask your partner to complete the pattern.

Experiment 19

How could you instruct someone over the telephone if you wanted him to reproduce this shape?

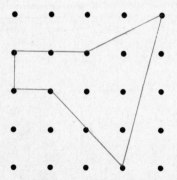

Give each corner of your figure a letter and then mark the bottom left-hand corner nail as the starting point, S.P.

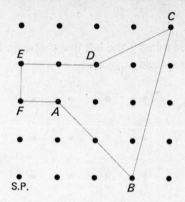

If the person on the other end of the telephone has a board numbered in the same way, you could then give instructions like this:

'Point *A*; 1 along and 2 up.'   'Point *B*; 3 along and 0 up.'

'Point *C*; 4 along and 4 up.'   'Point *D*; 2 along and 3 up.'

'Point *E*; 0 along and 3 up.'   'Point *F*; 0 along and 2 up.'

If you also agree between yourselves that you will always give the along-number first and the up-number second, the instructions become much simpler and might now be: *A* is (1, 2); *B* is (3, 0); *C* is (4, 4); *D* is (2, 3); *E* is (0, 3); *F* is (0, 2). Work in pairs. Take it in turns to make a shape without letting the other person see it and give instructions using this method. Compare the shapes you have obtained.

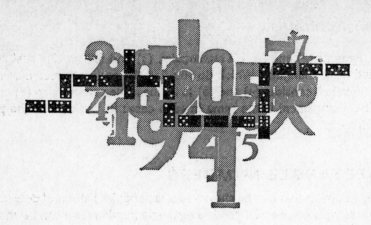

1. Number patterns

1. PATTERNS OF DOTS

How many dots are there in each pattern?

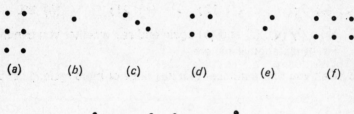

Did you have to count them or did you know the answers?

Make some dot patterns like these and show them quickly to your neighbour. Can he tell how many there are? Is it easier for him if the dots form a regular pattern?

Here are some of the ways we can arrange six dots to form a pattern.

7

Patterns (*a*) and (*b*) are rectangular, (*c*) and (*d*) are like straight lines and (*e*) is triangular. Which do you find the easiest to recognize as six?

We shall consider (*a*) and (*b*) to be the same pattern; also (*c*) and (*d*). The arrangement is the same in each case: its position on the page is different.

2. RECTANGLE NUMBERS

Any number that can be shown as a rectangular pattern of dots is called a *rectangle number*. Fifteen is a rectangle number for it can be shown as

Exercise A

1 Try these numbers and find out whether they will make rectangular patterns:

(*a*) 8;   (*b*) 3;   (*c*) 10;   (*d*) 18;
(*e*) 7;   (*f*) 12;   (*g*) 21;   (*h*) 20.

2 Now try (*d*), (*f*) and (*h*) again and see whether you can make a different rectangular pattern.

3 Can you find a number that has three or more rectangular patterns?

2.1 Finding the patterns

You will have found that you can only make rectangular patterns for certain numbers. All these rectangle numbers can be divided by numbers other than themselves and one.

We can see, for example, that twelve can be set out as

These patterns show 12 as 3×4 or as 2×6.

21 can be set out as

We know that $21 = 3 \times 7$.

Of course $12 = 3 \times 4 = 4 \times 3$. Though these patterns are the same, we shall make a point of stating the number of rows first, so

• • • •
• • • •   will be called a 3×4 rectangular pattern,
• • • •

• • •
• • •   a 4×3 rectangular pattern.
• • •
• • •

2, 3, 4 and 6 are called *factors* of 12.
3 and 7 are factors of 21.
Every rectangle number has its own set of factors.

Example 1

Find the factors of 48.

$$48 = 2 \times 24 \qquad 48 = 6 \times 8 \qquad 48 = 3 \times 16$$
$$48 = 4 \times 12 \qquad 48 = 1 \times 48$$

and even though the last two numbers do not give us a rectangular pattern, they do multiply together to give 48, so we include them in the set of factors.

The factors of 48 are 1, 2, 3, 4, 6, 8, 12, 16, 24 and 48.

When we are sure that we have found the whole set of factors of a number, we can write them like this:

$$\{\text{factors of 48}\} = \{1, 2, 3, 4, 6, 8, 12, 16, 24, 48\}.$$

The curly brackets are a short way of writing, 'The set of'.

{factors of 48} is read, 'The set of factors of 48', and this *describes* or *names* the set we are referring to.

{1, 2, 3, 4, 6, 8, 12, 16, 24, 48} is read 'The set 1, 2, 3, 4, 6, 8, 12, 16, 24, 48,' and this *lists* the *members* or *elements* of the set.

Example 2

Find {factors of 30}.

$$30 = 1 \times 30 \qquad 30 = 2 \times 15$$
$$30 = 3 \times 10$$
$$30 = 5 \times 6$$

$$\{\text{factors of 30}\} = \{1, 2, 3, 5, 6, 10, 15, 30\}.$$

9

In Example 1, we found quite a large number of factors for 48 and Example 2 shows us that 30 also has quite a lot. This could mean that with some numbers we may find it difficult to know when we have actually found all of them. The method of Example 2 will help us to do this.

We know that 1 will be a factor of all numbers, so we write that down first. Then we start with the next counting number, 2, and find out whether it is a factor. From there, go on to three, four, etc., until you have found them all.

Exercise B

1   Find the set of factors of each of the following numbers:

(*a*) 15;   (*b*) 27;   (*c*) 32;   (*d*) 46;   (*e*) 56;

(*f*) 63;   (*g*) 72;   (*h*) 81;   (*i*) 24;   (*j*) 33.

How did you know when to stop trying new numbers? Look at 36 again. When we try numbers to see whether they are factors we get: 1×36; 2×18; 3×12; 4×9; 6×6, and we have now found them all. If we did try to go on, the next result would be 9×4 and we already have these two factors. This shows that we can stop as soon as we come to two factors which are the same, or which repeat the previous pair. Look at 30 again. We get: 1×30; 2×15; 3×10; 5×6, and the next one will be 6×5, two numbers we have already.

3. SQUARE NUMBERS

3.1 A new pattern

We have already seen that some numbers have more than one pattern. Now we shall look at some special ones.

Example 3

Show 16 as a rectangle of dots in as many ways as possible.

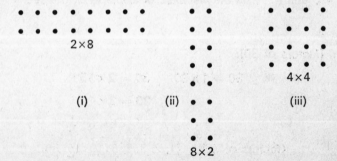

Two of the answers look very like those you have met already, but the third is a little different. There are the same number of rows as columns and so the pattern is a square of dots. Try to find three other numbers which can be represented by a square of dots. Such numbers are called *square numbers*.

To do this we had to find numbers which had two equal factors: $7 \times 7 = 49$; $6 \times 6 = 36$; $9 \times 9 = 81$; and a special one, $1 \times 1 = 1$.

'7×7' is often written as '7^2' which we read as '7 squared'. In the same way $16 = 4 \times 4 = 4^2$.

If we start at one, these numbers make a very interesting series of patterns:

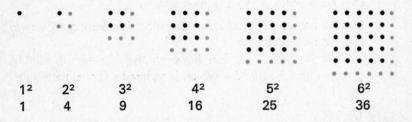

1^2	2^2	3^2	4^2	5^2	6^2
1	4	9	16	25	36

What are the next two numbers of this kind?

Notice that we have one square number which is not a rectangle number. Which is it?

We have shown the first six square numbers as a pattern of red and black dots. The red dots have been used to show how one square number is built up from the one before it.

Exercise C

1. (a) Draw a dot pattern for 3^2. By adding more dots, make it into a pattern for 4^2. How many dots did you add?
   (b) Using the same method, make 5^2 into 6^2. How many extra dots did you use?
   (c) Make 8^2 into 9^2. How many extra dots are needed?

2. Copy and complete the following:

$$2^2 = 1^2 + ?,$$
$$3^2 = 2^2 + 5,$$
$$4^2 = 3^2 + ?,$$
$$5^2 = ? + ?.$$

3. What relation is there between a square number and the square number before it?

4 The figure shows the square number 25 with lines drawn to divide the dots into different sets.

(a) By looking at the numbers of dots between the lines, and the number of dots in the square cut off by a particular line, complete the following:

$$1 = 1 = 1^2$$
$$1+3 = 4 = 2^2$$
$$1+3+5 = ? = 3^2$$
$$1+3+5+7 = 16 = ?$$
$$1+3+5+7+9 = ? = ?$$

(b) Now write down the next line.

5 Use the pattern of numbers in Question 4 to work out the sum of the first ten odd numbers.

What is the connection between the *number* of odd numbers summed and the *number* which is squared to equal their sum?

SUMMARY

A *factor* is a counting number which divides a whole number of times into another counting number.

Each *rectangle number* has more than two *factors*.

A *square number* is the product of two *equal factors*.

Miscellaneous Exercise D

1 (a) Draw as many rectangular patterns as you can for each of the following numbers:

(i) 18; (ii) 24; (iii) 30; (iv) 40; (v) 60.

(b) Now write down the set of factors of each of these numbers in turn.

2 (a) Draw as many rectangular patterns as you can for:

(i) 25; (ii) 36; (iii) 49; (iv) 64.

(b) Write down the set of factors of each of these numbers in turn.

3 (a) Use the relation between the numbers of odd numbers and the square numbers to find:

(i) $1+3+5+7 = ?$,

(ii) $1+3+5+7+9+11 = ?$,

(iii) $1+3+5+7+9+11+13+15+17+19 = ?$,

(iv) $1+3+5+7+9+\ldots+37+39 = ?$.

(b) What is $21+23+25+27+\ldots+37+39$?

4 Here are the first, second, .. odd numbers in order:

1st	2nd	3rd	4th	5th	...	50th	...	?
1	3	5	7	9	...	?	...	199

What numbers do the question marks stand for?
What is the 5000th odd number?

5 (*a*) What are the differences 3^2-2^2; 4^2-3^2; 5^2-4^2; 6^2-5^2?

(*b*) Complete the following:

The difference between

3^2 and 2^2 is the 3rd odd number which is 5;

5^2 „ 4^2 „ „ ? „ „ „ „ ?;

8^2 „ ? „ „ 8th „ „ „ „ ?;

11^2 „ ? „ „ ? „ „ „ „ ?;

? „ 10^2 „ „ ? „ „ „ „ ?;

? „ ? „ „ ? „ „ „ „ 199.

(*c*) $23^2 = 529$. Use the ideas of (*b*) to write down:

(i) the difference between 24^2 and 23^2;

(ii) 24^2.

6 The square of dots 2^2 can be split up by sloping lines like this

so you can see that $2^2 = 1+2+1$. In the same way

gives $3^2 = 1+2+3+2+1$. Use this pattern to complete the following:

(*a*)

1	$= 1^2$
$1+2+1$	$= 2^2$
$1+2+3+2+1$	$= 3^2$
$1+2+3+4+3+2+1$	$= ?$
$1+2+3+?+?+?+?+?+?$	$= ?$

(*b*) Write down the next three lines of the pattern.

2. Coordinates

1. BATTLESHIPS

You have probably played the game of Battleships before. First of all you want your fleet.

1 battleship (B)

2 cruisers (C)

3 destroyers (D)

4 motor torpedo boats (M)

Next you will need to make a plan of your fleet. To do this, draw on squared paper two blocks of 81 squares as shown in Figure 1.

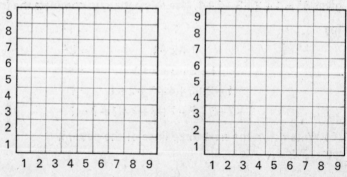

Fig. 1

One of these blocks will be for your own fleet, the other to mark your shots at the enemy's fleet. Mark the position of each ship of your own fleet as you wish. Remember that no ship can be bent, nor can two ships touch each other and that you must keep your plan secret from the enemy.

Here in Figure 2 is a game that has already been started. Each player has two plans as shown, one marked with his own fleet, and the other empty for marking his own shots at the enemy.

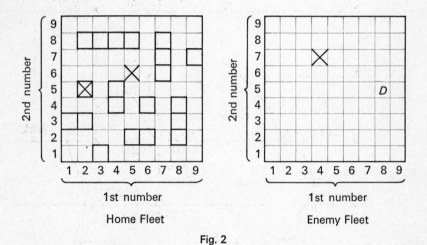

Fig. 2

Each player 'shoots' at the enemy by choosing two numbers which indicate the square on the plan in which his shot lands. The enemy shot at (2, 5) and has hit one of the Home Fleet's M.T.B.s. You must report this to the enemy so that he can mark it on his plan. The return shot at (4, 7) has hit nothing. The enemy then shot at (5, 6) and has drawn a blank. The Home Fleet's shot at (8, 5) has hit an enemy destroyer. It was marked D when the enemy admitted that his destroyer had been hit.

Now try the game with a friend in your class. Decide who will go first and then take it in turns to fire shots. The game continues until one fleet is completely destroyed.

2. MAPS

Figure 3 shows a map of 'Skull Island'. The map is divided into squares like the map you used for your fleet in the battleship game. Look at the bottom and the left-hand side of the map. There are numbers there as for battleships, but the numbers on this map have a different meaning. In the

Coordinates

game of battleships we numbered the spaces. On the map, it is the actual lines that are numbered. On our map, the lines show the number of kilometres east and north of a fixed point—the Old Wreck.

With the map we again describe the position of something by using two numbers. Do you think that the order in which this pair is written matters?

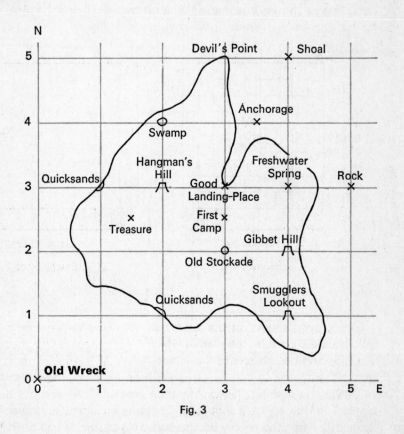

Fig. 3

It is usual to put the number of kilometres east first and the number of kilometres north second. So (4, 2) means four kilometres east and two kilometres north and therefore shows Gibbet Hill.

Exercise A

1 What places on the map are shown by the following pairs of numbers?

(a) (0, 0);   (b) (3, 3);   (c) (2, 1);   (d) (3, 2);

(e) (3, 5);   (f) (1, 3);   (g) (5, 3);   (h) (2, 3).

16

2   What pairs of numbers give the positions of the following places?

        (*a*) Smugglers' Lookout.
        (*b*) Shoal.
        (*c*) Swamp.
        (*d*) Freshwater Spring.
        (*e*) First Camp.
        (*f*) Anchorage.
        (*g*) Treasure.

3   Make up your own map. Choose a fixed point and draw the lines as in Figure 3. Mark in some interesting places and write down the pairs of numbers which give their positions.

3. PLOTTING POINTS

Have a look at Figure 4. This is rather like the pattern of lines on the map in Figure 3. Exactly as on the map, points can be indicated by using two numbers. In the same way as you yourself have a first and second name, so each point has a first and second name. Look at the point *A* in Figure 4. Its first name is 2 and its second name is 3. So its full name is (2, 3). Look at the point *B*. Its first name is 5 and its second name is 2. So its full name is (5, 2).

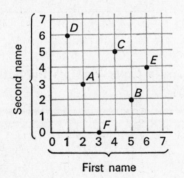

Fig. 4

What are the full names of *C, D, E, F*?

We usually call the full name of a point its *'coordinates'*. So the coordinates of *A* are (2, 3) and the coordinates of *B* are (5, 2).

What are the coordinates of *C, D, E, F*?

Notice that it is usual to take the first name from the set of numbers across the page. The second name comes from the set of numbers up the page.

Coordinates

Exercise B

1

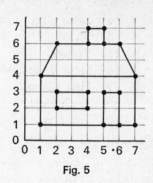

Fig. 5

Figure 5 shows a house. What are the coordinates of

(a) the top of the chimney;   (b) the corners of the window;
(c) the corners of the door;   (d) the corners of the roof?

2

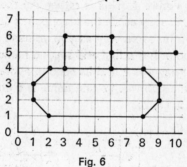

Fig. 6

Figure 6 shows a tank. What are the coordinates of the points marked in black?

3

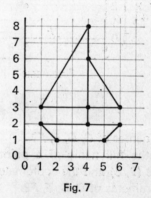

Fig. 7

Figure 7 shows a sailing boat. What are the coordinates of the points marked in black?

4 Plot on squared paper the set of points with the following coordinates. Join them up in the order in which they are written. What pictures do you get?

(*a*) (2, 1), (6, 1), (6, 3), (7, 3), (4, 6), (1, 3), (2, 3);

(*b*) (1, 1), (5, 1), (5, 6), (4, 7), (4, 11), (3, 13), (2, 11), (2, 7), (1, 6);

(*c*) (1, 1), (3, 1), (4, 3), (5, 3), (5, 5), (6, 5), (5, 7), (5, 9), (1, 9).

In (*c*), what should be put round the point (4, 7)?

5 Plot on squared paper the sets of points with the following coordinates. Which capital letters of the alphabet do they suggest?

(*a*) (1, 1), (2, 3), (3, 5), (4, 3), (5, 1), (3, 3);

(*b*) (4, 0), (4, 2), (2, 4), (6, 4);

(*c*) (1, 4), (2, 2), (3, 0), (4, 2), (5, 4);

(*d*) (1, 4), (1, 3), (1, 2), (1, 1), (2, 1), (3, 1);

(*e*) (1, 1), (2, 1), (3, 2), (3, 3), (2, 4), (1, 4), (1, 2½).

6 Plot on squared paper the following pairs of points and join up each pair with a straight line. What are the coordinates of the middle point of each of these lines?

(*a*) (1, 4), (1, 6); (*b*) (5, 2), (1, 2); (*c*) (2, 3), (6, 5);

(*d*) (2, 5), (0, 0); (*e*) (6, 0), (0, 2); (*f*) (7, 3), (2, 7);

(*g*) (7, 6), (4, 1); (*h*) (1, 2), (3, 8); (*i*) (6, 3), (2, 4).

Look at the coordinates of the end-points of each line and the coordinates of the middle point of that line. Can you find any connection between the two? Can you now give a rule for finding the coordinates of the middle point of a line?

7 Draw the line joining (0, 6) and (6, 4) and also the line joining (4, 7) and (1, 1). Where do they meet?

8 Make up a picture that can easily be described by the coordinates of its corners. Read out the coordinates to your neighbour. See if he can plot them correctly and discover what you have drawn. Now it is your turn to discover his picture.

4. LINES

Look at Figure 8. What do you notice about the points *I*, *J* and *F*? What do you notice about their first names? Are there any other points whose first names are also 3? Have you got the point half-way between *I* and *J*? Are you sure you have *all* the points whose first names are 3?

Coordinates

In mathematics we call the first name (the first coordinate) of a point, the x-coordinate. We can call the whole line

$$x = 3.$$

As this expression has an equals sign, we call this the *equation* of the line.

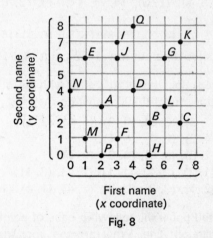

Fig. 8

Look at the points *B* and *H*. What are the x-coordinates of *B* and *H*? What are the x-coordinates of all the other points on the same line? Give the 'equation', that is the mathematical description, of the line.

Look at the points *E*, *J* and *G*. What do you notice about their first names? What do you notice about their second names? In mathematics we call their second names their y-coordinates. Are there other points which have the same y-coordinate? As the y-coordinate of all the points of this line is 6, the mathematical name or equation of this line is

$$y = 6.$$

Look at the points *B* and *C*. What are the y-coordinates of *B* and *C* and all the other points on the same line? What is the equation of this line?

Exercise C

What are the equations of the lines on which the following points in Figure 8 lie?

1 *L* and *G*.

2 *M* and *E*.

3 *N* and *D*.

4 *I* and *K*.

5 *P* and *A*.

6 *A* and *L*.

7 *K* and *C*.

8 *Q* and *D*.

9 *M* and *F*.

10 *P* and *H*.

20

The lines $x = 0$ and $y = 0$ are called the 'axes'. The point O, where they intersect, is called the 'origin'. What are the coordinates of the origin? See Figure 9.

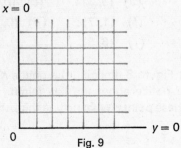

Fig. 9

This figure shows the axes with the coordinates marked along them, also the lines $x = 3$ and $y = 2$ which intersect at A. What are the coordinates of A?

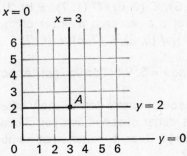

Fig. 10

The coordinates of A are given by the ordered pair (3, 2). Will the ordered pair (2, 3) give the point at A? What do we mean by 'ordered pair'?

Is it difficult to mark the point R in Figure 10 at (2, 5)?. This is easy to do, but what about the points (9, 3) or (2, $4\frac{1}{2}$) or ($1\frac{3}{4}$, 5)?

Can we mark in any point we like?

Exercise D

1   The lines $x = 2$ and $y = 3$ intersect at the point (2, 3). At what points do the following lines intersect?

(a) $x = 3$, $y = 2$;   (b) $x = 5$, $y = 6$;   (c) $x = 4$, $y = 4$;

(d) $y = 1$, $x = 2$;   (e) $x = 3$, $x = 4$;   (f) $y = 1$, $y = 5$;

(g) $x = 1$, $y = 6$;   (h) $y = 0$, $x = 5$;   (i) $x = 2$, $y = 7$;

(j) $x = 2$, $y = 4$.

2 The point (3, 1) lies on the lines $x = 3$ and $y = 1$.
On what lines do the following points lie?

(*a*) (2, 4);   (*b*) (5, 3);   (*c*) (0, 1);   (*d*) (3, 0);
(*e*) (4, 4);   (*f*) (1, 7);   (*g*) (0, 0);   (*h*) (6, 9);
(*i*) (7, 8);   (*j*) (6, 3).

3 Look back at Figure 8. Imagine the points *K*, *G*, *D* and *M* joined up. What do you notice about the line joining them? Look at the co-ordinates of these points. What do you think the equation of this line is?

5. REGIONS

On squared paper, mark with a dot each member of the set of points *A* (2, 5), *B* (1, 3), *C* (0, 6), *D* (1, 7), *E* (0, 2), *F* (2, 1). On the same paper mark with a cross each member of the set of points *G* (4, 6), *H* (6, 0), *I* (4, 1), *J* (5, 3), *K* (7, 5), *L* (6, 7).

Draw in the line $x = 3$. What do you notice about the two sets of points?

Where could you put more dots to show other points belonging to the first set? Does it matter what numbers you choose for their 'x-coordinates' (their first names)? Does it matter what numbers you choose for their 'y-coordinates'?

Where could you put more crosses to show other points belonging to the second set? Does it matter what you choose for their x-coordinates? Does it matter what you choose for their y-coordinates?

Where do you think you could NOT put any dots or crosses?

The line $x = 3$ separates the plane into two sets of points called *regions*. Are there any points that do not belong to either region? What about the points actually on the line itself?

So there are really three sets:
(i) points on one side of the line,
(ii) points on the other side of the line,
(iii) points on the line.

For the region containing the set of dots, you found that, while the y-coordinates could be anything you liked, all the x-coordinates were less than 3. This is written for short as '$x<3$'. This is the mathematical description of the region.

For the region containing the set of crosses, you found that while again the y-coordinates could be anything you liked, all the x-coordinates were bigger than 3. This is written for short as '$x>3$'.

Look at the points A to L again. Find all the points marked whose y-coordinates are bigger than 4. Put a circle round each of them. What is the mathematical description of the region which contains these points?

Can you find all the points marked whose y-coordinates are less than 4? Put a square round each of them. What is the description of the region that contains these points?

What is the equation of the line which separates the two regions?

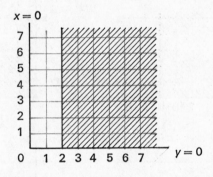

Fig. 11

In Figure 11 the points have been divided into two regions by a line. What is this line called? Look at the shaded region. Look at the x numbers marked along the bottom in this region. Is this the region $x < 2$ or $x > 2$? Look at the x numbers marked along the bottom in the unshaded region. Is this the region $x < 2$ or $x > 2$?

Sketch Figure 11 and mark the line $y = 3$ with a thick line. By looking at the y numbers along the side, decide which is the region $y > 3$ and then shade it in. What is the other region called?

Exercise E

1 Name the shaded regions in Figure 12:

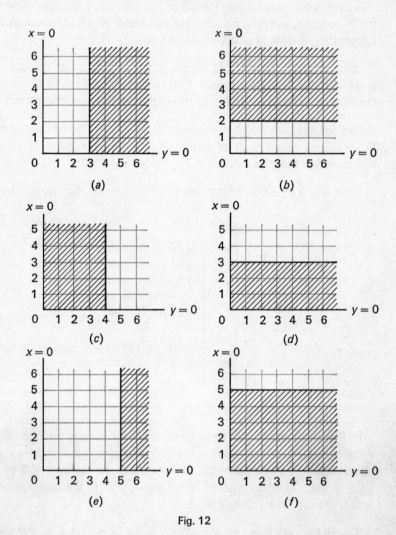

Fig. 12

2 By sketching diagrams similar to Figure 12, show the regions:

(a) $x > 4$; (b) $y > 1$; (c) $x < 3$; (d) $y < 2$;

(e) $y > 4$; (f) $x < 1$; (g) $x > 1$; (h) $y < 4$;

(i) $x > 0$; (j) $y > 0$; (k) $3 < x$; (l) $5 > y$;

(m) $4 < y$; (n) $5 > x$; (o) $2 < x$.

3

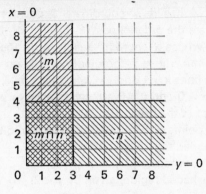

Fig. 13

Figure 13 shows two regions *m* and *n*. What are they? The overlap of the two regions has a special name. It is called '*m* intersection *n*' and is written as '*m* ∩ *n*'.

4   Let *p* be the region *x* > 2. On a diagram shade in the region *p*. Let *q* be the region *y* > 4. On the same diagram shade differently the region *q*. Mark in the region *p* ∩ *q* (that is where *p* and *q* overlap).

5   Let *r* be the region *x* > 4, *s* the region *y* < 3 and *t* the region *x* < 6.
(*a*)   On the same diagram, show, by different shadings, the regions *r* and *s*. Mark in the region *r* ∩ *s*.
(*b*)   On another diagram, show, by different shadings, the regions *s* and *t*. Mark in the region *s* ∩ *t*.
(*c*)   Do the same for *r* and *t*.

SUMMARY

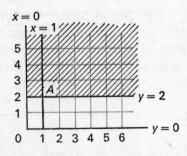

Fig. 14

We arrange the axes so that the *x*-coordinate of a point is taken from the set of numbers across the page and the *y*-coordinate from the set of numbers up the page.

25

The point A has its x-coordinate 1 and its y-coordinate 2. So its coordinates are the ordered pair (1, 2).

All points whose x-coordinate is 1 lie on the line whose equation is $x = 1$. All points whose y-coordinate is 2 lie on the line whose equation is $y = 2$. The lines $x = 1$ and $y = 2$ intersect at A, the point (1, 2).

The lines $x = 0$ and $y = 0$ are called axes or base lines of the system. They intersect at the origin (0, 0).

The set of points on Figure 14 is divided into three:

(i)   the shaded region, given by $y > 2$;
(ii) the line, whose equation is $y = 2$;
(iii) the unshaded region, given by $y < 2$.

Miscellaneous Exercise F

1 Plot the following sets of points. What capital letters of the alphabet do they suggest?

(a) (1, 4), (1, 2), (1, 0), (2, 2), (3, 2), (4, 4), (4, 2), (4, 0);

(b) (1, 4), ($2\frac{1}{2}$, 4), (4, 4), ($2\frac{1}{2}$, 3), ($2\frac{1}{2}$, 2), ($2\frac{1}{2}$, 1).

2 (a) At what point do the lines $x = 4$ and $y = 5$ intersect?
   (b) What lines intersect at the point (3, 3)?

3 Plot the points (3, 2) and (3, 5). What is the equation of the line on which they lie? Shade in the region $x > 3$. What is the unshaded region called?

4 Let r be the region $x > 1$ and s the region $y > 3$. Show by shading the region $r \cap s$.

5 See if you can play the game of Submarines. This game is slightly more difficult than that of Battleships but very similar to it. With submarines of course we have to go under the water, so we need a third coordinate to give the depth below the surface. The game is played on 4 layers of 16 squares each, as in Figure 15, each layer being one unit deeper than the previous one.

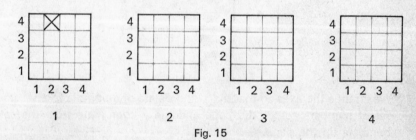

Fig. 15

Each fleet is as follows:

1 polaris submarine

3 killer submarines

5 midget submarines

The game is now played exactly like Battleships, each player taking it in turn to fire depth charges. A cross has been put to show a depth charge exploding at (2, 4, 1).

6   You will have played noughts and crosses on many occasions and may have exhausted all the possibilities, knowing how to win or how not to lose! We can extend the game into three dimensions.

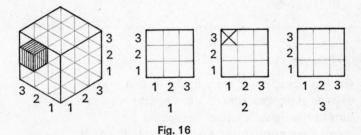

Fig. 16

Instead of 9 squares we have 27 squares such that each set of 9 squares is thought of as a layer: a bottom layer, a middle layer and a top layer. (Think of a building with 9 rooms on the ground floor, 9 on the first floor and 9 on the top floor.) The × is shown in the position (1, 3, 2). The object of the game is to obtain not only one set of three ×'s or ○'s in a line but as many as possible. Examples of winning lines are

$$(3, 3, 1), \quad (3, 3, 2), \quad (3, 3, 3);$$
$$(1, 3, 1), \quad (1, 2, 2), \quad (1, 1, 3);$$
$$(3, 1, 1), \quad (2, 2, 2), \quad (1, 3, 3).$$

3. Angles

Experiment 1

On the floor, draw a north–south line and an east–west line crossing it. Stand at the centre and turn to the right or left, as instructed.

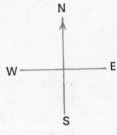

Fig. 1

(*a*) Face north, make a whole turn to the right, three whole turns to the left, two whole turns to the right. In what direction were you facing after each set of turns?

(*b*) Notice in which direction you are facing at the end of each of the following movements.

(i) Face east, make a half-turn to the left.
(ii) Face north, make a quarter-turn to the right.
(iii) Face south, make a three-quarter turn to the left.
(iv) Face west, make one-and-a-half turns to the left.

Would you be facing in the same direction after each movement if you had turned the opposite way by mistake?

(*c*) Draw the lines as before but add the north–east—south–west and the north–west—south–east lines.

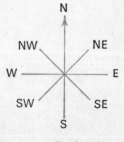

Fig. 2

You make a one-eighth turn in turning from any one line to the next. In what direction would you be facing after each of the following turns?

Face east, make one-eighth turn left.

Face south–west, make one-half turn to the right.

Face south, make five-eighths of a turn to the left.

28

1. ROTATIONS

We often turn things or parts of things. Already today you will probably have

> turned a door knob to open a door;
> turned a door on its hinges;
> turned a water tap on and off;
> screwed and unscrewed the cap of a toothpaste tube;
> turned your head to look at the person beside you;
> turned your whole body when moving about the house.

(*a*) What other things can you think of that turn, rotate, revolve or spin?

(*b*) What is the difference between the movements needed to turn the tap on and to turn it off?

When we rotate things we sometimes have to be careful how much we rotate them. In adjusting the hands of a watch we have to be quite exact in the amount we twist the winder. Many things have marks on them to help us to judge the amount of a turn; the numbers on the knobs of a cooker or television set or radio, for example. Name some other objects on which dials or knobs are marked to show an amount of turn.

A *rotation* is the mathematical name for a turn. A rotation has a centre of rotation, a direction of rotation and a size of rotation.

The point marked with a red dot is the centre of rotation of the illustrations in Figures 3, 4 and 5. In the examples of the door knob, toothpaste tube or when you turn, there is always a hub or axis at the centre of the turn.

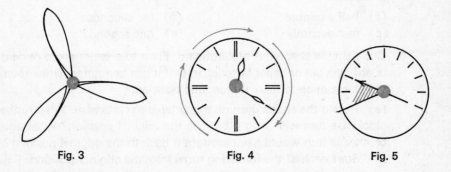

Fig. 3   Fig. 4   Fig. 5

The direction of rotation is indicated with reference to a clock (see Figure 4). It can be clockwise or anticlockwise.

For the time being, we shall use a whole-turn as the basic unit for measuring the size of a rotation. The needle of the dial of Figure 5 has moved through an eighth turn.

Angles

Exercise A

1 Experiment to discover the direction of turn and its size, to the nearest half-turn, when you carry out the following actions. Give a rough description of the centre of rotation in each case.

(a) Unlock your front door.
(b) Screw or unscrew the top of the toothpaste tube.
(c) Turn the volume knob of the radio or T.V. set fully on.
(d) Dial 9 on a telephone.
(e) Turn the cold tap of the bath fully on (and fully off).

2 The minute hand of a clock goes through a whole turn each hour. What part of a turn does it make in:

(a) 2 hours; (b) 5 hours; (c) $3\frac{1}{2}$ hours; (d) $\frac{1}{2}$ hour;
(e) $\frac{1}{4}$ hour; (f) 20 min; (g) 45 min; (h) 5 min.?

3 What time passes when:

(a) the minute hand rotates through a quarter-turn;
(b) the hour hand rotates through one whole turn;
(c) the hour hand rotates through a quarter-turn;
(d) the second hand rotates through a half-turn?

4 A sewing machine makes 3 stitches for every turn of the flywheel. How much does the flywheel turn when the machine makes:

(a) 6 stitches; (b) 15 stitches; (c) 1 stitch; (d) 2 stitches?

5 A record makes 45 revolutions per minute. How many times does it revolve in:

(a) half a minute; (b) ten seconds;
(c) four seconds; (d) one second?

6 Cut a simple shape out of cardboard. Fix it to a larger piece of cardboard by a pin or paper fastener so that it can be rotated. Draw round the shape once to mark the original position.

(a) Rotate the shape through a quarter-turn clockwise. What further clockwise turn will bring it back to the original position? What anti-clockwise turn would have brought it back to the original position?

(b) Start each of the following turns from the original position. Four of them will bring you to the same new direction. Which one is the exception?

   (i) A quarter-turn clockwise;
   (ii) a three-quarter turn anticlockwise;
   (iii) a half-turn clockwise;
   (iv) two-and-a-quarter turns clockwise;
   (v) one-and-three-quarter turns anticlockwise.

30

(*c*) Starting from the original position, make first a quarter-turn clockwise then a three-quarter turn anticlockwise. Starting again from the original position, reverse the order of these turns. Are you facing in the same direction after both experiments?

Try doing other turns first in one order and then in another. Does the order ever make any difference to the final direction?

2. CORNERS AND ANGLES

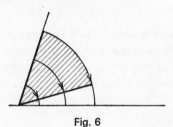

Fig. 6

An object moving along a line, moves through a *distance*. An object, rotating about a point, rotates through an *angle*. The angles we have met so far have been measured in turns or fractions of a turn. In turning from north to east, you rotate through an angle called a 'quarter-turn'.

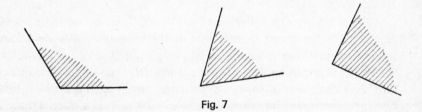

Fig. 7

One way of comparing the pointedness of these corners is by comparing the angles at the corners. A pencil set on one line of the corner can be rotated about the point of the corner until it lies on the other line. The amount of rotation is an indication of the pointedness of the corner: the bigger the rotation, the less pointed the corner.

A searchlight set in the corner between two walls can be turned to shine along one wall. Then it can be turned until it shines along the other. The amount of rotation is a measure of the angle between the walls (see Figure 8).

When cutting lino, a knife is drawn along to the point of the corner and is then turned through the angle marked in red and drawn away from the corner. The angle of the shaded piece of lino together with the angle of

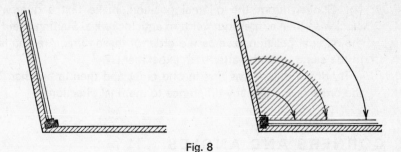

Fig. 8

the knife turn make a half-turn. When you are walking along the side of a building and then turn a corner, the amount by which you turn added to the angle of the corner of the building, makes a half-turn. When cutting out some material with scissors, the angle turned by the scissors at the corner together with the angle of the piece of material cut out, make a half-turn. See Figure 9.

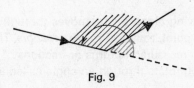

Fig. 9

In Figure 10, any one of the lines *OA*, *OB* or *OC* may be rotated clockwise or anticlockwise about *O* onto one of the other lines. We shall some-times refer to these rotations as 'the angles at *O*' and call the point *O* the *vertex* of these angles. (The sentence 'Draw an angle of a quarter-turn,' is a short way of saying 'Draw two lines in such a position that if one is rotated onto the other, the angle of rotation is a quarter-turn.')

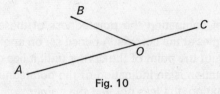

Fig. 10

To distinguish the various angles at *O*, we shall use the notation $\angle AOB$ to indicate the angle obtained by rotating *OA* onto *OB*; or $\angle BOC$ to indicate the angle obtained by rotating *OB* onto *OC*. (In each case, it is the smaller of the two possible rotations that is referred to.)

When *AOC* is a straight line we can write that

$$\angle AOB + \angle BOC = \text{a half-turn.}$$

Exercise B

1 Sketch an angle for each rotation:

(a) $\frac{1}{4}$ turn left;   (b) $\frac{1}{8}$ turn right;   (c) $\frac{3}{4}$ turn right;

(d) $\frac{1}{6}$ turn left;   (e) $\frac{5}{8}$ turn left;   (f) $\frac{3}{8}$ turn right.

2 What is special about these angles:

(a) a half-turn right or left;

(b) a whole-turn right or left?

3 The corner of Figure 11 is $\frac{1}{6}$ turn. Trace it to help you draw the angles:

(a) $\frac{1}{6}$ turn right;

(b) $1\frac{1}{6}$ turn right;

(c) $\frac{1}{6}$ turn left;

(d) $2\frac{1}{6}$ turn left;

(e) $3\frac{1}{6}$ turn right.

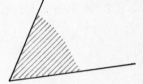

Fig. 11

4 Through what angle do you turn in going,

(a) from south clockwise to west;

(b) from north-west clockwise to north-east;

(c) from north clockwise to south-east;

(d) from north-west anticlockwise to south;

(e) from north-east anticlockwise to south-east?

5 Describe these angles:

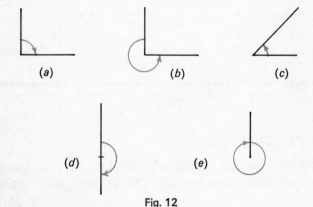

Fig. 12

6 A clock face shows twelfths of a whole-turn.
    Draw these angles:

(a) $\frac{1}{12}$ turn clockwise;   (b) $\frac{9}{12}$ turn anticlockwise;

(c) $\frac{11}{12}$ turn clockwise;   (d) $\frac{2}{12}$ turn clockwise;

(e) $\frac{4}{12}$ turn anticlockwise;   (f) $\frac{7}{12}$ turn anticlockwise.

33

7 These wedges of cheese have slightly different angle sizes. Give them in order from the smallest angle to the largest.

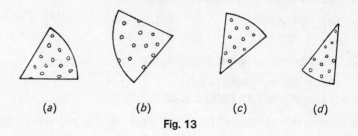

(a)   (b)   (c)   (d)

Fig. 13

8 A man is fitting lino at this corner of a floor.

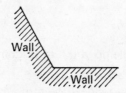

Which of these pieces would fit the corner?

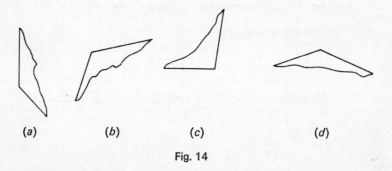

(a)   (b)   (c)   (d)

Fig. 14

3. RIGHT-ANGLES

When a line is rotated through a quarter-turn the angle formed is called a *right*-angle. Right-angles are often marked with square marks.

It is often unnecessary to show the direction of turn and, from now on, we shall sometimes not mark the direction of the angle.

There is a method of making an accurate right-angle without measuring the rotation. Take a piece of paper (or cloth or a leaf) and fold it once. Then fold it again, as in the picture, so that *A* meets *B*.

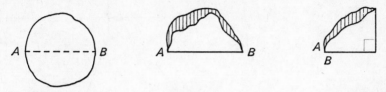

Fig. 15

You have divided a whole turn into quarters and made four right-angles. When you unfold the paper you can see that the angle about any point on a straight line is two right-angles. Two straight lines that cross at right-angles are said to be *perpendicular* to each other.

Look for some examples of right-angles. You should be able to count at least 200 of them in a day.

We can compare other angles with right-angles.

An *acute* angle is an angle less than a right-angle.

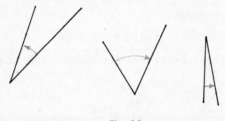

Fig. 16

An *obtuse* angle is an angle greater than one right-angle but less than two right-angles.

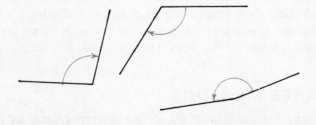

Fig. 17

A *reflex* angle is an angle greater than two right-angles but less than four right-angles (see Figure 18).

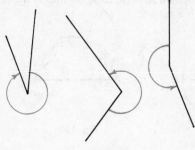

Fig. 18

Exercise C

1   Which angles are acute? Which angles are obtuse? Which angles are reflex?

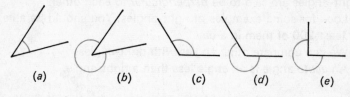

(a)   (b)   (c)   (d)   (e)

Fig. 19

2   Sketch these angles:

(a) 3 right-angles;   (b) $\frac{1}{2}$ right-angle;   (c) $\frac{3}{4}$ right-angle.

3   Which of these pairs of lines are perpendicular to each other?

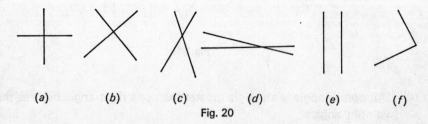

(a)   (b)   (c)   (d)   (e)   (f)

Fig. 20

(a)   Give six examples of pairs of perpendicular lines.

(b)   What is meant by a *vertical* line? What is meant by a *horizontal* line? Is a vertical line always perpendicular to a horizontal line?

4. DEGREE MEASURE

The early Babylonians (three to two thousand years B.C.) were great astronomers, and needed accurate measurements to describe the movements of the planets. They probably based their units on one-sixth of a turn, which they split into sixtieths (they were particularly interested in sixties), and called 'degrees'.

60° (read 'sixty degrees') is a sixth of a whole turn.

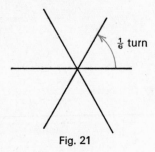

Fig. 21

(*a*) How many degrees is a whole turn?
(*b*) How many degrees is half a turn?
(*c*) How many degrees is a right-angle?
(*d*) How many degrees is a one-twelfth turn?
Here is an angle of 1 degree.

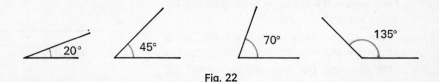

Here are some angles with their size shown in degrees.

20° 45° 70° 135°

Fig. 22

(*e*) Use the above angles to estimate the size of the following ones in degrees.

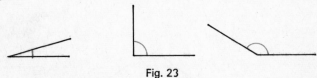

Fig. 23

(*f*) Make sketches to illustrate angles that are roughly of these sizes:

90°, 60°, 45°, 180°, 110°.

4.1 Use of protractor

To draw and measure angles accurately we need an instrument called a '*protractor*' (see Figure 24). The angle sizes are marked in degrees.

37

Angles

It is usually semi-circular and made of transparent plastic. The idea is to compare the angle marked on the protractor with that on the paper.

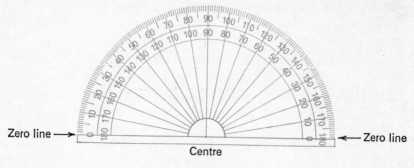

Fig. 24

This protractor has two scales. The outer scale goes 0⌢180° clockwise; the inner scale goes 180°⌢0 anticlockwise.

(a) To measure the angle *BOC*, place the centre of the protractor over the vertex *O*.

Fit the right-hand zero line over the line *OC*. Note where the line *OB* cuts the inner scale—the one whose zero is on *OC*. Why would it have been wrong to use the outer scale in this case?

We could have measured the same angle by putting the left-hand zero line over the line *OB* and noting where *OC* cuts the outer scale.

Here is another angle measured in two ways.

Fig. 25

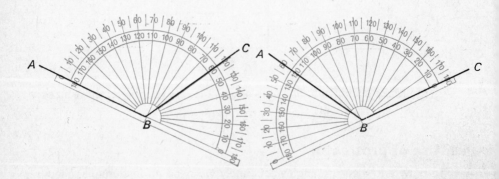

Fig. 26

Since even the best of us occasionally read from the wrong scale, you should check your answer by seeing whether the angle is obtuse or acute, whether it 'looks right'.

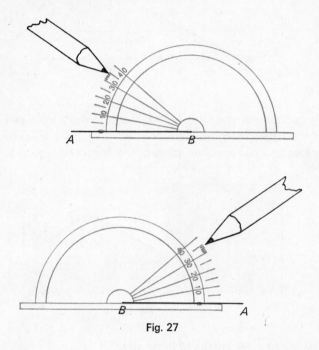

Fig. 27

(*b*) To draw an angle *ABC* of 34° mark the vertex *B*, and draw a line from it, ending at *A*. Place the centre of the protractor on *B*, and a zero line along *BA*. On the scale with this zero line find 34, and make a dot. Remove the protractor, and join the dot to *B*.

Make sure the angle you have drawn looks about the right size.

(*c*) How would you measure a reflex angle?

Exercise D

1   Measure the marked angles of this figure with your protractor.

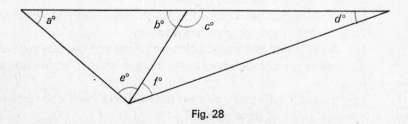

Fig. 28

39

2 Measure the following angles of the given figure: ∠BAD; ∠BDC; ∠ABC.

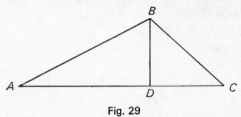

Fig. 29

3 Trace the outline of this figure. Measure the angles which are in the shaded part of the silhouette. You may have to extend the sides before you can measure some of the angles with your protractor.

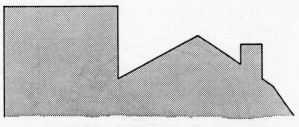

Fig. 30

4 Draw and mark angles of these sizes:

(*a*) 25°; (*b*) 44°; (*c*) 90°;
(*d*) 61°; (*e*) 120°; (*f*) 167°.

5 Draw two straight lines at the following angles as accurately as you can without using a protractor. (In time, you should be able to judge angles to within 20° by eye.) Check the angles with a protractor.

(*a*) 90°; (*b*) 60°; (*c*) 45°; (*d*) 30°; (*e*) 6°;
(*f*) 70°; (*g*) 120°; (*h*) 150°; (*i*) 100°; (*j*) 135°.

6 (*a*) A car has turned through a quarter-turn on its way round a round-about. Through how many degrees has it turned?
(*b*) A ship changes course clockwise from north to south-west. Through how many degrees has it turned?
(*c*) A girl is nibbling round a circular biscuit and has one-sixth of the distance to go. Through how many more degrees must the biscuit be turned?
(*d*) Through how many degrees does an hour hand of a clock move between two and three o'clock?

7 In the following diagrams, right-angles and some other angles are marked. Calculate (do not use your protractor) the size of the angles marked with small letters.

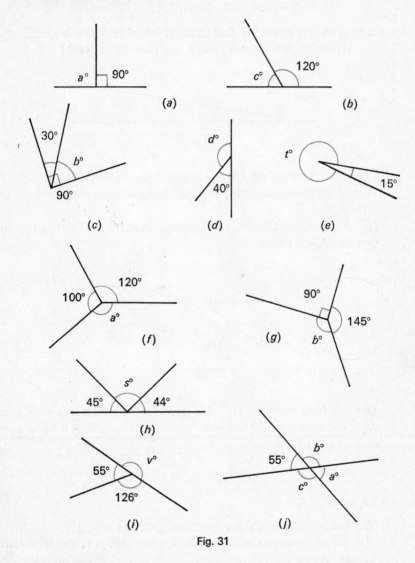

Fig. 31

8 (a) What is the sum of two angles , ∠AOB and ∠BOC at O, if AC is a straight line? (Such angles are called *'supplementary'* angles.)
(b) If two angles that are supplementary have a vertex and one line in common, what can you say about the other two lines?
(c) Two angles, ∠AOB and ∠BOC, together form a right-angle. (They are said to be *'complementary'*.) Is OA perpendicular to OC?

(*d*) Here are two sets of angles:

$$A = \{10°, \ 55°, \ 75°, \ 100°, \ 145°\};$$

$$B = \{35°, \ 80°, \ 105°, \ 125°, \ 170°\}.$$

For each angle in set *A*, find its supplementary angle in set *B*.

(*e*) Which angles in set *A* have a complement in set *B*?

9 (*a*)

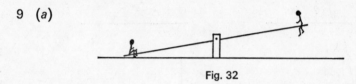

Fig. 32

Copy the picture of the seesaw in which the beam moves through 20°. Through what angle do the children turn? About what point are they rotating?

(*b*) *Experiment.* Draw the following curves on the floor so that they can be walked round.

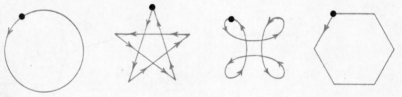

Fig. 33

Through how many whole turns have you rotated if you walk round each of these curves? Measure the amount which you have turned *only in one direction*.

5. TRIANGLES

(*a*) On a sheet of paper, draw three straight lines which:
(i) do not intersect at all and which are always the same distance apart (parallel);
(ii) intersect at only one point;
(iii) intersect at just two points;
(iv) intersect at three points.

Can you draw three straight lines which intersect at four points?

The figure formed when three straight lines intersect at three points is called a *triangle*. (Three angles.)

(*b*) Mark three points on a sheet of paper and join them with straight lines. What can you say about the position of the three points if the resulting figure is not a triangle?

(*c*) Draw a triangle with one obtuse angle. Can you draw a triangle with two obtuse angles? Can you draw a triangle with two right-angles?

What is the greatest number of acute angles that a triangle can have? What is the smallest number?

(*d*) Make a frame by threading cotton through four drinking straws. Can you alter the angles of the frame without bending or breaking the straws? Repeat the experiment, this time making a triangular frame. Can you alter the angles of the triangular frame?

The triangle is said to form a 'rigid' framework. How could you make the square rigid?

Engineers use the fact that a triangle forms a rigid framework in some of their constructions. Railway bridges, signal frames and some crane structures are examples.

(*e*)

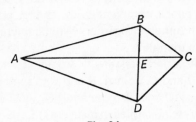

Fig. 34

A triangle is named using the three points that are its vertices. *ABC* is a triangle of this figure. Name the other seven.

(*f*) (i) Draw many different shaped triangles and measure their inside angles. What would be your estimate of the sum of the angles of a triangle? Would this be true of all triangles?

(ii) Draw a triangle and cut it out. Tear off the corners and arrange them as shown below. What do you notice about the sum of the angles at these corners? Does this agree with your estimate in (i)?

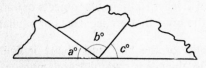

Fig. 35

(iii)

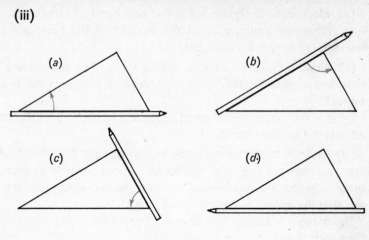

(a)

(b)

(c)

(d)

Fig. 36

Place a pencil along one side of a triangle and turn it about each vertex in order as shown in the diagram. What do you notice about the final position of the pencil compared with its first position? Through what angle has it been turned altogether? What can you say about the sum of the angles of the triangle?

(g) Draw a circle and mark any two points on it. Call the centre A, and the two points, B and C. Join A, B and C to form a triangle and measure the sides AB and AC and also the angles ∠ABC and ∠ACB. (Is there a case where there are no angles to measure?) Repeat the construction with different sizes of circle and with different positions for B and C. The sides AB and AC will always be the same length. What can you say about the angles opposite these equal sides?

A triangle with two equal sides is called *isosceles*.

Would you expect a triangle with two equal angles also to have equal sides? Construct some triangles with equal angles and see.

The length BC could be made to equal the length of the other two sides. This special isosceles triangle is called an *equilateral* triangle. What is the size of each angle of an equilateral triangle?

Exercise E

1   Make a list of at least 10 triangular objects or frameworks that you have seen. Note the ones that are isosceles or equilateral.

2   Draw triangles of the size and shape indicated on the following diagrams. Do this very carefully and measure the other sides and angles in each case.

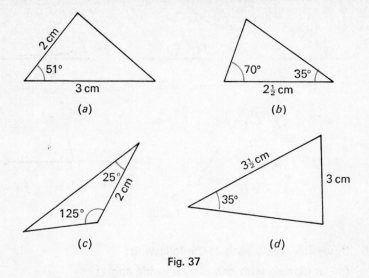

Fig. 37

3 Assuming that the three angles of a triangle add up to 180°, work out the size of the third angle in the following triangles:

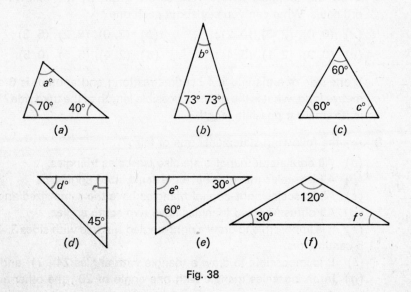

Fig. 38

4 Work out the size of the angle marked with a letter in each of the cases in Figure 39. Try to find a direct connection between the lettered angle and the two given angles in each case.

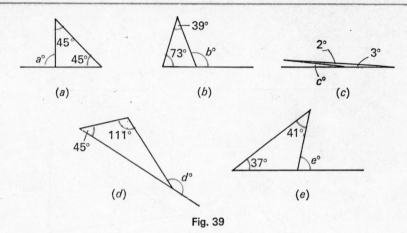

Fig. 39

5 If possible, draw each of the following:

(*a*) a triangle with one obtuse inside angle;
(*b*) a triangle with two obtuse inside angles;
(*c*) a triangle with two right-angles;
(*d*) a triangle with three acute angles.

6 Draw the triangles whose vertices are given by the following co-ordinates. What can you say about each one?

(*a*) (0, 0), (2, 0), (0, 2);   (*b*) (3, 0), (6, 2), (5, 3);
(*c*) (0, 3), (2, 1), (5, 4);   (*d*) (2, 4), (5, 5), (0, 5).

7 If one side of a triangle is 4 centimetres long and another is 6 centimetres long, what is the greatest possible length of the third side? What is its smallest possible length?

8 Are the following statements true or false?

(*a*) All equilateral triangles are also isosceles triangles.
(*b*) All isosceles triangles have the same sized angles.
(*c*) All isosceles right-angled triangles have the same sized angles.
(*d*) All obtuse-angled triangles have two acute angles.
(*e*) It is impossible to draw a right-angled triangle with sides 3, 4 and 5 centimetres.
(*f*) It is impossible to draw a triangle with angles 24°, 71° and 63°.
(*g*) In an isosceles triangle with one angle of 20°, the other angles must both be 80°.
(*h*) All three angles of an equilateral triangle are the same size.
(*i*) Three different triangles can be drawn with one angle of 20°, another of 30° and one side 8 centimetres long.

4. Number bases

1. COUNTING NUMBERS

1.1 Counting

How many stars are there?

To answer this question, we have to count. When we count the number of objects in a collection, we mentally tick off each object against this list:

1, 2, 3, 4, 5, 6, 7, 8, 9, ...

We can think of this list as showing a series of equal steps along a line.

1, 2, 3, 4, 5, 6, 7, 8, 9, ...

We can place the stars along the line like this:

1, 2, 3, 4, 5, 6, 7, 8, 9, ...

Because the last star is beside the '7', we say that there are 'seven' stars in the group. There will be times when we go to count a set of objects and find that there are none. So we shall add '0' to our set of numbers on the line which will now look like this:

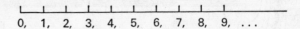

0, 1, 2, 3, 4, 5, 6, 7, 8, 9, . . .

Do the symbols that we use make any difference to the position of the last star along the number line? Is this position altered if we write different numerals along the line? Here are some examples of other systems of numerals:

	1	2	3	4	5	10	12
Babylonian	۷	۷۷	۷۷۷	۷۷ ۷۷	۷۷۷ ۷۷	⟨	⟨۷۷
Egyptian hieratic	I	II	III	۱۱۱۱	۹	ٮ	ٮII
Early Roman	I	II	III	IIII	V	X	XII
					or		
					∧		

Invent a series of number symbols for yourself and give them names. Try counting collections of objects so that you get used to your own system. Now use your system to add and subtract.

1.2 Addition and subtraction

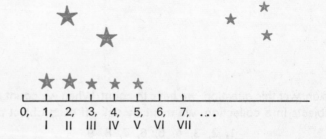

0, 1, 2, 3, 4, 5, 6, 7, . . .
I   II III IV V VI VII

From the picture, you can see that whatever symbol you use in the addition, the actual number of stars remains unaffected. Did you find that your symbol for '3' plus your symbol for '2' came to your symbol for '5'? See if your system works for other additions.

If there are six planes on an airstrip and two take off, there will be four left. We write

$$6 - 2 = 4.$$

On the number line this would be shown as

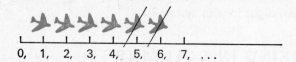

0, 1, 2, 3, 4, 5, 6, 7, ...

Can you subtract using your system of symbols?

1.3 Multiplication

Multiplication is a short way of counting objects when we have several groups of them that are all the same size.

This flight of geese is in three groups, each of five birds. If we mark these off in groups along the number line, we would have

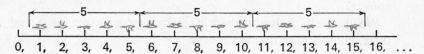

0, 1, 2, 3, 4, 5, 6, 7, 8, 9, 10, 11, 12, 13, 14, 15, 16, ...

We have repeatedly added fives together. In number symbols this repeated addition is written

$$5+5+5 = 15.$$

However, it is quicker to learn and remember that three lots of five come to fifteen ($3 \times 5 = 15$), and so we have our multiplication tables.

Just as multiplication is repeated addition, so division may be thought of as repeated subtraction. If we start with twelve dogs and take them off in pairs for a walk, the number of walks we would have to take would be given by twelve divided by two. On the number line, this can be shown as

0, 1, 2, 3, 4, 5, 6, 7, 8, 9, 10, 11, 12, 13, ...

Can you use *your* system to carry out multiplication and division? Do the symbols that you have used affect the actual number of stars, planes, geese or dogs?

49

What is it about the standard number system that makes it so generally used? Why is it that the next numbers after nine have two digits? Did they have two digits in your system?

2. WORKING IN COLUMNS

The text and exercises in Section 2 involve the use of imperial units.

2.1 Addition

Which of these is correct? Add them up and see.

$$(a) \quad + \begin{array}{cc} 4 & 7 \\ 3 & 9 \\ \hline 8 & 4 \end{array} \qquad (b) \quad + \begin{array}{cc} 4 & 7 \\ 3 & 9 \\ \hline 8 & 0 \end{array} \qquad (c) \quad + \begin{array}{cc} 4 & 7 \\ 3 & 9 \\ \hline 8 & 6 \end{array}$$

You have probably found that (c) is right, but in fact all three could be.

In (a) put feet and inches as column headings.

In (b) put pounds and ounces as column headings.

In (c) put tens and units as column headings.

Now add up and check again.

Can you think of any other column headings which would make (a) correct?

We usually think that numbers in columns represent hundreds, tens, and units, but this need not be the case.

Exercise A

1 Find column headings which will make these additions correct:

(a)	2 8	(b)	2 8	(c)	2 8	(d)	2 9
	1 9		1 9		1 9		3 7
	4 5		4 1		4 7		6 0

(e)	2 9	(f)	4 9	(g)	2 2	(h)	2 3
	3 7		3 5		1 2		5 8
	6 2		8 2		4 1		8 1

(i)	3 4	(j)	3 4	(k)	4 4	(l)	8 6
	2 6		2 6		1 4		4 2
	6 3		6 2		6 1		12 8

(m)	3 8	(n)	2 8	(o)	5 2
	2 8		7		3 2
	6 0		3 1		9 1

2.2 Subtraction

It is not so easy to discover the column headings if they are missing from a subtraction.

(*a*) Try this:

$$\begin{array}{r} 6\ \ 2 \\ -\ 1\ \ 9 \\ \hline 4\ \ 5 \\ \hline \end{array}$$

You would start by saying '2, take away 9'. This cannot be done, but the next idea should help to make things easier.

Take an easy example first:

$$\begin{array}{r} 7 \\ -\ 5 \\ \hline 2 \\ \hline \end{array}$$

You can always check a subtraction by adding together the answer and the number you took away; this should give you the number you started with.

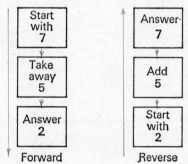

Start with 7		Answer 7
Take away 5		Add 5
Answer 2		Start with 2
Forward		Reverse

See how this works with:

$$\begin{array}{r} t\ \ u \\ 4\ \ 7 \\ -\ 2\ \ 9 \\ \hline 1\ \ 8 \\ \hline \end{array} \quad \text{which becomes} \quad \begin{array}{r} t\ \ u \\ 1\ \ 8 \\ +\ 2\ \ 9 \\ \hline 4\ \ 7 \\ \hline \end{array}$$

So you see, we can always check a subtraction question by turning it into an addition question.

(*b*) Find column headings for this subtraction question by reversing and then checking the addition:

$$\begin{array}{r} 4\ \ 2 \\ -\ 2\ \ 9 \\ \hline 1\ \ 7 \\ \hline \end{array} \quad \text{can be written as} \quad \begin{array}{r} 1\ \ 7 \\ +\ 2\ \ 9 \\ \hline 4\ \ 2 \\ \hline \end{array}$$

51

which should show you that you are dealing with stones and pounds, so put in the column headings and check,

$$
\begin{array}{r}
\text{st} \quad \text{lb} \\
4 \quad 2 \\
- \quad 2 \quad 9 \\
\hline
1 \quad 7 \\
\hline
\end{array}
$$

Exercise B

1   Find the missing numbers:

(a)
$$
\begin{array}{r}
\text{t} \quad \text{u} \\
? \quad ? \\
- \quad 1 \quad 3 \\
\hline
2 \quad 5 \\
\hline
\end{array}
$$

(b)
$$
\begin{array}{r}
\text{t} \quad \text{u} \\
? \quad ? \\
- \quad 3 \quad 6 \\
\hline
4 \quad 1 \\
\hline
\end{array}
$$

(c)
$$
\begin{array}{r}
\text{t} \quad \text{u} \\
? \quad ? \\
- \quad 4 \quad 7 \\
\hline
2 \quad 8 \\
\hline
\end{array}
$$

(d)
$$
\begin{array}{r}
\text{t} \quad \text{u} \\
? \quad ? \\
- \quad 5 \quad 6 \\
\hline
3 \quad 6 \\
\hline
\end{array}
$$

2   Find the column headings:

(a)
$$
\begin{array}{r}
4 \quad 2 \\
- \quad 2 \quad 9 \\
\hline
1 \quad 5 \\
\hline
\end{array}
$$

(b)
$$
\begin{array}{r}
5 \quad 4 \\
- \quad 2 \quad 7 \\
\hline
2 \quad 5 \\
\hline
\end{array}
$$

(c)
$$
\begin{array}{r}
2 \quad 0 \\
- \quad 1 \quad 1 \\
\hline
1 \\
\hline
\end{array}
$$

(d)
$$
\begin{array}{r}
2 \quad 2 \\
- \quad 1 \quad 6 \\
\hline
3 \\
\hline
\end{array}
$$

2.3 Multiplication

Multiplication is a shorthand for repeated addition and the same ideas can be used as in Section 2.1.

Exercise C

1   Find the column headings:

(a)
$$
\begin{array}{r}
2 \quad 7 \\
\times \quad 3 \\
\hline
7 \quad 5 \\
\hline
\end{array}
$$

(b)
$$
\begin{array}{r}
2 \quad 7 \\
\times \quad 3 \\
\hline
7 \quad 9 \\
\hline
\end{array}
$$

(c)
$$
\begin{array}{r}
2 \quad 7 \\
\times \quad 3 \\
\hline
7 \quad 1 \\
\hline
\end{array}
$$

(d)
$$
\begin{array}{r}
2 \quad 7 \\
\times \quad 3 \\
\hline
7 \quad 7 \\
\hline
\end{array}
$$

(e)
$$
\begin{array}{r}
2 \quad 7 \\
\times \quad 3 \\
\hline
8 \quad 1 \\
\hline
\end{array}
$$

(f)
$$
\begin{array}{r}
1 \quad 6 \\
\times \quad 3 \\
\hline
5 \quad 4 \\
\hline
\end{array}
$$

(g)
$$
\begin{array}{r}
1 \quad 2 \\
\times \quad 2 \\
\hline
3 \quad 0 \\
\hline
\end{array}
$$

(h)
$$
\begin{array}{r}
2 \quad 6 \\
\times \quad 4 \\
\hline
9 \quad 8 \\
\hline
\end{array}
$$

(i)
$$
\begin{array}{r}
1 \\
\times \quad 5 \\
\hline
21 \\
\hline
\end{array}
$$

(j)
$$
\begin{array}{r}
3 \\
\times \quad 5 \\
\hline
11 \\
\hline
\end{array}
$$

2.4 Division

Division is more difficult but, just as with subtraction, we can find a way round it. Take an easy example first.

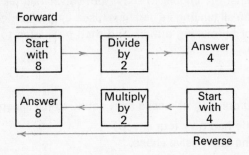

We can use this idea to find the column headings for:

$$6\overline{)7\ 6}^{\,1\ 3}, \quad \text{by changing the question into} \quad \begin{array}{r} 1\ 3 \\ \times\ \ \ 6 \\ \hline 7\ 6 \end{array}$$

and you should now see that it could be feet and inches.

Exercise D

1 Find the missing numbers:

   (*a*)   t u   (*b*) t u   (*c*)   t u

           3 2   1 4   1 9

       $3\overline{)?\ ?}$ $6\overline{)?\ ?}$ $5\overline{)?\ ?}$

2 Find the column headings:

   (*a*) $6\overline{)7\ 4}^{\,1\ 4}$ (*b*) $6\overline{)7\ 4}^{\,1\ 2}$ (*c*) $6\overline{)7\ 4}^{\,1\ 3}$

   (*d*) $4\overline{)5\ 1}^{\,1\ 1}$ (*e*) $5\overline{)7\ 1}^{\,1\ 3}$

3. GROUPING

3.1 Base ten

All the examples so far were meant to remind you that numbers in columns really need headings. It is the custom to leave out the headings when we are working in tens.

Why is it that we normally count things in groups of ten? Nobody knows for certain, but it seems very likely that it is because we have ten fingers and people use their fingers to count with.

Early man would come out of his cave in the morning and tally his sheep against his fingers to see if the wolves had taken any sheep overnight. When all ten fingers had been used up, he 'carried' this fact either in his head or by making a mark and then he started to use his fingers all over again.

Exercise E

1   Make a drawing of a cave man counting his sheep,

   (*a*) if he had only four sheep;
   (*b*) if he had twelve sheep.

3.2 Other bases

Things might have been very different if man had only one arm with five fingers on the hand. Then he would have to record every group of five instead of every group of ten.

This number of sheep   would be thought of as

or as

The 'one' that was carried stood for a group of five units. Writing this in number symbols we could put 12.

But 12 might be confused with twelve, so we must read it as 'one two' and write it either as

Fives	Units
1	2

or, more neatly, as 12_{five}.

In future work we shall use this method and call it *base five*.

Exercise F

1   Copy these patterns of dots. Count them in base ten, then group into fives and write the answers in number symbols to base five.

(*a*)

(*b*)

(*c*)

(*d*)

(*e*)

(*f*)

2 Show these base five numbers as groups of dots.

(*a*) 14₅;   (*b*) 20₅;   (*c*) 33₅;

(*d*) 41₅;   (*e*) 104₅.

4. THE SPIKE ABACUS

All the ideas of this section need to be illustrated by using a spike abacus. This is so important that it is worth making one, even roughly, if there are none ready to be used.

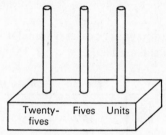

4.1 Using the spike abacus

We shall use the spike abacus to count in fives. Mark the spikes 'units', 'fives', 'twenty-fives'.

As you count, go on adding rings to the units spike until you get:

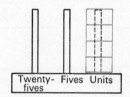

If you try to add another, there is no spike left for it to go on, so 'carry' one ring on to the fives spike and clear the units:

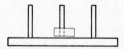

Start all over again on the units spike and continue until you reach:

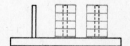

You should now have counted twenty-four. If you now try to add another to the units spike you have to carry one to the fives spike, but this is full up also, so you will carry again and end up with:

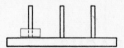

What is the greatest number you can represent on this spike abacus?

Exercise G

1 Copy this table into your book and complete it. Do this by counting the rings on to the spike abacus.

	Base ten	Base five
a	7	
b	14	
c	26	
d	38	
e	57	
f	100	

2 Load the abacus with rings to show these numbers in base five and count them in base ten as they are removed.

	Base ten	Base five
a		11
b		3
c		40
d		34
e		111
f		322

Copy this table into your book and complete it.

4.2 Operation tables

(*a*) Add the following numbers in base five and give their sum in the same base. If necessary, use your abacus.

$$+\begin{matrix}1\\1\end{matrix} \quad +\begin{matrix}1\\2\end{matrix} \quad +\begin{matrix}1\\3\end{matrix} \quad +\begin{matrix}1\\4\end{matrix} \quad +\begin{matrix}2\\2\end{matrix} \quad +\begin{matrix}2\\3\end{matrix} \quad +\begin{matrix}2\\4\end{matrix} \quad +\begin{matrix}3\\3\end{matrix} \quad +\begin{matrix}3\\4\end{matrix} \quad +\begin{matrix}4\\4\end{matrix}$$

(*b*) We can use these results to make out an 'operations' table for addition of numbers written in base five.

+	0	1	2	3	4
0	0	1	2	3	4
1	1	2	3	4	10
2	2	3	4	10	11
3	3	4	10	11	12
4	4	10	11	12	13

Copy the table into your book for reference. Can you see any patterns among the numbers of the table?

(*c*) We can use this table for subtraction in the following way:

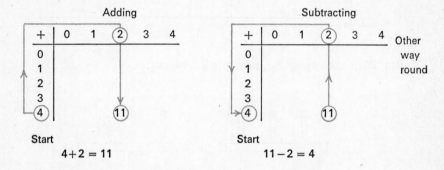

Adding

$4+2 = 11$

Subtracting

$11-2 = 4$

Check all the entries in the table with your spike abacus.

Exercise H

Perform the following additions and subtractions where all the numbers are in base five and give your answers in base five also. Use the operation table where necessary.

1 (*a*) $+$ 14
  3

(*b*) $+$ 12
  4

(*c*) $+$ 23
  3

(*d*) $+$ 4
  33

(*e*) $+$ 32
  2

(*f*) $+$ 31
  20

(*g*) $+$ 44
  1

(*h*) $+$ 124
  11

(*i*) $+$ 213
  22

(*j*) $+$ 231
  41

(*k*) $+$ 343
  24

(*l*) $-$ 23
  12

(*m*)	10	(*n*)	14	(*o*)	33	(*p*)	42
−	2	−	11	−	14	−	13
	—		—		—		—

Do not forget to check your subtractions by addition. (See the method used in Section 2.2.)

4.3 Subtraction with the spike abacus

A situation such as 34_{five} take away 12_{five} is straightforward:

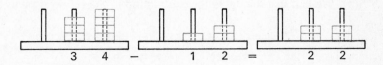

But, 31_{five} take away 3_{five} presents a problem:

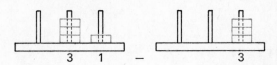

There is only one ring on the units spike and you want to remove three units. 'One take away three' cannot be done. To overcome this difficulty we have to use one of the rings on the fives spike and exchange it for five units:

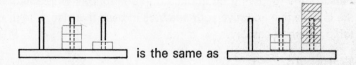

is the same as

The five shaded rings represent the five-ring which has been removed. Now the problem is solved:

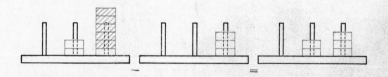

The answer is 23_{five}.

Exercise I

Draw spike abacus diagrams to represent the steps to be taken to carry out these base five subtractions.

1 (a) 23−4;

(b) 30−12;

(c) 41−33;

(d) 233−42;

(e) 321−34;

(f) 432−234.

4.4 Multiplying in base five

Multiplying in base five should present no problems.

Exercise J

All these numbers are written in base five. Give the answers in base five.

1 (a) $\times$ $\begin{array}{r} 3 \\ 2 \\ \hline \\ \hline \end{array}$

(b) $\times$ $\begin{array}{r} 4 \\ 2 \\ \hline \\ \hline \end{array}$

(c) $\times$ $\begin{array}{r} 4 \\ 3 \\ \hline \\ \hline \end{array}$

(d) $\times$ $\begin{array}{r} 12 \\ 2 \\ \hline \\ \hline \end{array}$

(e) $\times$ $\begin{array}{r} 13 \\ 2 \\ \hline \\ \hline \end{array}$

(f) $\times$ $\begin{array}{r} 21 \\ 3 \\ \hline \\ \hline \end{array}$

(g) $\times$ $\begin{array}{r} 12 \\ 4 \\ \hline \\ \hline \end{array}$

(h) $\times$ $\begin{array}{r} 23 \\ 3 \\ \hline \\ \hline \end{array}$

(i) $\times$ $\begin{array}{r} 43 \\ 4 \\ \hline \\ \hline \end{array}$

(j) $\times$ $\begin{array}{r} 12 \\ 11 \\ \hline \\ \hline \end{array}$

(k) $\times$ $\begin{array}{r} 23 \\ 12 \\ \hline \\ \hline \end{array}$

(l) $\times$ $\begin{array}{r} 134 \\ 23 \\ \hline \\ \hline \end{array}$

Copy this multiplication table into your book and complete it. A few of the entries have already been made, to start you off.

×	0	1	2	3	4
0	0	0	0		
1					
2					
3	0				14
4			13		

Look for patterns

The multiplication table can be used to give answers to division questions just as the addition table helped with subtraction.

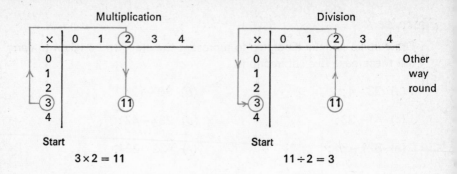

Multiplication	Division

$3 \times 2 = 11$ $11 \div 2 = 3$

Exercise K

All these numbers are in base five. Give the answers in base five.

1 (a) $2\overline{)\,13}$ (b) $4\overline{)\,22}$ (c) $4\overline{)\,13}$

  (d) $4\overline{)\,31}$ (e) $2\overline{)\,11}$ (f) $3\overline{)413}$

4.5 Using an extra spike

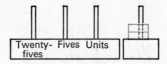

Start counting with the spike abacus by putting rings on the extra spike first. This time you will have to use five rings to get the position below.

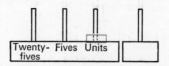

We have called the right-hand spike the 'extra one'. What is a better name for it? Remember, five on this spike are needed to make a whole one.

Call this the 'one-fifth' spike; rings placed upon it each represent the fraction one-fifth.

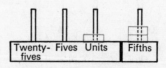

This situation represents one and two-fifths.

Exercise L

The questions of this exercise are written in base ten. Give the answers in base ten.

What numbers are represented by these situations?

1   2   3

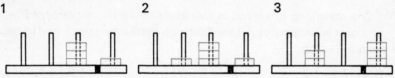

Draw diagrams to illustrate the positions on a base five abacus for:

4   (a) $2\frac{2}{5}$;   (b) $5\frac{1}{5}$;   (c) $14\frac{3}{5}$.

Use your spike abacus to do these:

5   (a) $3\frac{1}{5}+1\frac{2}{5}$;   (b) $2\frac{3}{5}+1\frac{4}{5}$;   (c) $4\frac{4}{5}+2\frac{3}{5}$;

    (d) $3\frac{1}{5}-2\frac{2}{5}$;   (e) $4\frac{1}{5}-\frac{2}{5}$;   (f) $3\frac{2}{5}-1\frac{4}{5}$.

4.6 The fraction point

The number shown on this abacus is $2\frac{1}{5}$. This can be more neatly written as $2 \cdot 1_{\text{five}}$ using a dot to represent the band on the abacus. The dot is placed level with the middle of the digits.

Questions 1–3 of Exercise L can now be written as

$$3 \cdot 1_{\text{five}} \qquad 13 \cdot 1_{\text{five}} \qquad 20 \cdot 3_{\text{five}}.$$

The dot is read 'point' and a numeral such as $4 \cdot 1$ would be read 'four point one'. The dot is sometimes called a 'fraction point'.

Exercise M

These numbers are in base ten. Write them in base five using a fraction point.

1 (a) $4\frac{1}{5}$;   (b) $3\frac{2}{5}$;   (c) $1\frac{4}{5}$;

   (d) $1\frac{1}{5}$;   (e) 2;   (f) $\frac{3}{5}$.

Now work the other way round. These numbers are in base five, put them back to base ten writing out the fractions:

2 (a) 3·2;   (b) 4·1;   (c) 3·3;

  (d) 2·0;   (e) 1·4;   (f) 0·2.

The remaining questions in this exercise are written in base five. Add, and give your answers in base five with the fraction point *and* in base ten with a fraction:

3 (a) 2·1+1·2;   (b) 4·3+0·1;   (c) 1·3+2·1.

Subtract, and give your answers in base five with the fraction point and in base ten with a fraction:

4 (a) 3·4−2·3;   (b) 0·4−0·1;   (c) 4·4−3·0.

Add and give your answer in the fraction point method.

5 (a) $+\begin{array}{r} 2·2 \\ 1·4 \\ \hline \\ \hline \end{array}$ (b) $+\begin{array}{r} 2·3 \\ 1·3 \\ \hline \\ \hline \end{array}$ (c) $+\begin{array}{r} 3·3 \\ 3·4 \\ \hline \\ \hline \end{array}$

  (d) $+\begin{array}{r} 1·4 \\ 4·1 \\ \hline \\ \hline \end{array}$ (e) $+\begin{array}{r} 13·2 \\ 3·1 \\ \hline \\ \hline \end{array}$ (f) $+\begin{array}{r} 20·3 \\ 41·4 \\ \hline \\ \hline \end{array}$

Subtract and give your answer in the fraction point method.

6 (a) $-\begin{array}{r} 3·1 \\ 2·1 \\ \hline \\ \hline \end{array}$ (b) $-\begin{array}{r} 4·3 \\ 2·4 \\ \hline \\ \hline \end{array}$ (c) $-\begin{array}{r} 32·3 \\ 4·1 \\ \hline \\ \hline \end{array}$

  (d) $-\begin{array}{r} 21·2 \\ 3·0 \\ \hline \\ \hline \end{array}$ (e) $-\begin{array}{r} 231·3 \\ 40·1 \\ \hline \\ \hline \end{array}$ (f) $-\begin{array}{r} 320·3 \\ 11·2 \\ \hline \\ \hline \end{array}$

Did you check all your subtractions by the method we used before?

4.7 Bases four and six

There was no special reason for choosing base five. If you think of the original idea of grouping which we used, you will see that we can count in any number as a base.

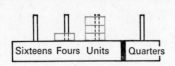

Sixteens Fours Units | Quarters

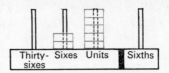

Thirty-sixes Sixes Units | Sixths

A base four abacus
showing
13_{four}

What is this in base ten?

A base six abacus
showing
25_{six}

What is this in base ten?

You can easily alter your base five abacus to these or any other bases by pulling out the spikes and replacing them with ones of the desired height.

Exercise N

1 Copy and complete this table.

	Base ten	Base four	Base five	Base six	
a	7				
b	10				When in
c		30			doubt
d	29	131	104	45	refer to
e			33		your
f			202		abacus
g				53	
h				105	
i		303			
j				111	

2 Copy and complete these tables in base four.

+	0	1	2	3
0				
1				
2				
3				

×	0	1	2	3
0				
1				
2				
3				

3 Copy and complete these tables in base six.

+	0	1	2	3	4	5
0						
1						
2						
3						
4						
5						

×	0	1	2	3	4	5
0						
1						
2						
3						
4						
5						

4 All in base four,

(*a*) $+\begin{array}{r} 22 \\ 2 \end{array}$ (*b*) $+\begin{array}{r} 101 \\ 23 \end{array}$ (*c*) $+\begin{array}{r} 23 \\ 12 \end{array}$ (*d*) $-\begin{array}{r} 32 \\ 13 \end{array}$

(*e*) $-\begin{array}{r} 123 \\ 30 \end{array}$ (*f*) $\times\begin{array}{r} 12 \\ 2 \end{array}$ (*g*) $\times\begin{array}{r} 203 \\ 3 \end{array}$ (*h*) $\times\begin{array}{r} 332 \\ 12 \end{array}$

5 All in base six,

(*a*) $+\begin{array}{r} 34 \\ 13 \end{array}$ (*b*) $+\begin{array}{r} 205 \\ 24 \end{array}$ (*c*) $+\begin{array}{r} 333 \\ 34 \end{array}$ (*d*) $-\begin{array}{r} 44 \\ 5 \end{array}$

(*e*) $-\begin{array}{r} 320 \\ 24 \end{array}$ (*f*) $\times\begin{array}{r} 12 \\ 3 \end{array}$ (*g*) $\times\begin{array}{r} 421 \\ 4 \end{array}$ (*h*) $\times\begin{array}{r} 224 \\ 21 \end{array}$

4.8 Using fixed scales to add and subtract

Here is another device to help you work in base five:

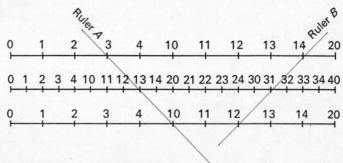

Copy these scales into your book

To add two numbers together, find one number on the top scale and the other on the bottom. Lay a ruler across and the answer will appear on the middle scale.

Ruler *A* shows: $3_{five}+10_{five}=13_{five}$,
Ruler *B* shows: $14_{five}+12_{five}=31_{five}$.

Exercise O

1 Perform these base five additions with the aid of the adding scales:

(*a*) $13+14$; (*b*) $2+11$; (*c*) $4+13$; (*d*) $14+14$.

2 See if you can 'work backwards' and use the scales to do these:

(*a*) 4−1;　　　　　(*b*) 12−4;　　　　　(*c*) 30−14.

3 Explain how you would use the scales to subtract.

4 Study the scales and see if you can see how they were made. See if you can make other scales which will work in:

(*a*) base four;　　　(*b*) base six;　　　(*c*) base ten.

4.9 Multiplication by the base

In everyday base ten arithmetic, to multiply by ten is very simple. Multiplication by ten just moves every number over to the next place on the left and we put a nought to fill the empty space.

For example:

$$
\begin{array}{ccccccccc}
h & t & u & & t & u & & h & t & u \\
1 & 7 & \times & 1 & 0 & = & 1 & 7 & 0
\end{array}
$$

Will there be the same sort of rule in other bases?

What happens if you multiply a base five number by five?

What happens if you multiply a base eight number by eight?

Exercise P will help you answer these questions.

Exercise P

First do the question in base ten, then change it into the given base and do it again.

The first two have been done for you as examples:

	Question (base ten)	Answer	Base	Question	Answer
	23 ×5	115	Five	43 ×10	430
	11 ×7	77	Seven	14 ×10	140
1	7 ×5		Five		
2	7 ×3		Three		
3	13 ×4		Four		
4	33 ×5		Five		
5	9 ×6		Six		
6	8 ×7		Seven		
7	11 ×8		Eight		
8	21 ×9		Nine		

Can you now make up a general rule which applies whenever you multiply a number, written in a certain base, by that base?

Number bases

Miscellaneous Exercise Q

1 Add: 5 weeks 3 days, 1 week 2 days and 1 week 6 days.

2 Add: 2 years 5 months, 1 year 8 months and 7 months.

3 Put in column headings to make these correct.

(a)
$$+\begin{array}{r}25\\16\\\hline 43\end{array}$$

(b)
$$+\begin{array}{r}41\\21\\\hline 70\end{array}$$

(c)
$$+\begin{array}{r}12\\12\\\hline 31\end{array}$$

(d)
$$+\begin{array}{r}39\\19\\\hline 52\end{array}$$

(e)
$$+\begin{array}{r}28\\18\\\hline 42\end{array}$$

(f)
$$+\begin{array}{r}35\\34\\\hline 72\end{array}$$

(g)
$$\times\begin{array}{r}13\\3\\\hline 42\end{array}$$

(h)
$$\times\begin{array}{r}13\\3\\\hline 51\end{array}$$

(i)
$$\times\begin{array}{r}12\\3\\\hline 50\end{array}$$

(j)
$$-\begin{array}{r}64\\58\\\hline 8\end{array}$$

(k)
$$-\begin{array}{r}71\\42\\\hline 22\end{array}$$

(l)
$$-\begin{array}{r}22\\9\\\hline 19\end{array}$$

4 Count these dots in the usual base ten manner, then group into sixes and represent the situation in number symbols to base six.

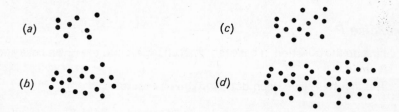

(a)

(c)

(b)

(d)

5 Write down in words the meaning of 40_{six}. Why is the 0 there?

6 Have you noticed that in base five only the symbols, or digits, 0, 1, 2, 3 and 4 are used? What are the digits we can use in:

(a) base four; (b) base seven; (c) base nine; (d) base ten?

7 What does the 4 mean in 43 if it is in:

(a) base ten; (b) base six; (c) base eight?

What is the lowest base 43 can be written in?

8 Write down the number of these dots

(a) in base ten; (b) in base four; (c) in base five.

9 Copy and complete these addition and multiplication squares for base eight.

+	0 1 2 3 4 5 6 7
0	
1	
2	
3	
4	
5	
6	
7	

×	0 1 2 3 4 5 6 7
0	
1	
2	
3	
4	
5	
6	
7	

10 All in base eight.

(a) $+\begin{array}{r}27\\12\\\hline\end{array}$ (b) $+\begin{array}{r}45\\25\\\hline\end{array}$ (c) $+\begin{array}{r}26\\17\\\hline\end{array}$ (d) $+\begin{array}{r}127\\44\\\hline\end{array}$

(e) $+\begin{array}{r}205\\63\\\hline\end{array}$ (f) $+\begin{array}{r}343\\52\\\hline\end{array}$ (g) $-\begin{array}{r}32\\5\\\hline\end{array}$ (h) $-\begin{array}{r}52\\14\\\hline\end{array}$

(i) $-\begin{array}{r}74\\47\\\hline\end{array}$ (j) $\times\begin{array}{r}12\\5\\\hline\end{array}$ (k) $\times\begin{array}{r}34\\2\\\hline\end{array}$ (l) $\times\begin{array}{r}46\\2\\\hline\end{array}$

11 Copy and complete:

	Base ten	Base five	Base six	Base eight
a	9			
b	12			
c	20			
d		20		
e			21	
f				20
g		140		
h			201	
i				34
j				121

12 Write these in a different form:

(a) $2 \cdot 1_{\text{four}}$;   (b) $3 \cdot 3_{\text{four}}$;   (c) $0 \cdot 2_{\text{four}}$;

(d) $3 \cdot 1_{\text{six}}$;   (e) $1 \cdot 5_{\text{six}}$;   (f) $0 \cdot 3_{\text{six}}$;

(g) $2 \cdot 7_{\text{eight}}$;   (h) $4 \cdot 5_{\text{eight}}$;   (i) $0 \cdot 3_{\text{eight}}$.

Number bases

13 The clues are in the bases as shown but the answers are to be written in base ten.

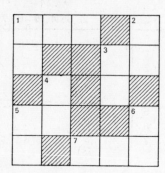

Across

1. 411_{five}
3. 33_{four}
5. 42_{eight}
7. 300_{six}

Down

1. 23_{four}
2. 300_{five}
3. 15_{seven}
4. 136_{eight}
5. 40_{nine}
6. 44_{six}

14 Copy and complete this set of adding scales for base eight.

15 Use the scales you drew for Question 14 to answer these:

(a) $13_{eight} + 17_{eight}$;

(b) $23_{eight} + 23_{eight}$;

(c) $46_{eight} - 27_{eight}$.

68

5. Symmetry

1. INK DEVILS

Many different patterns can be made using folded paper—sometimes the results are surprising but, if you are both quick and careful, you may be able to design a pattern.

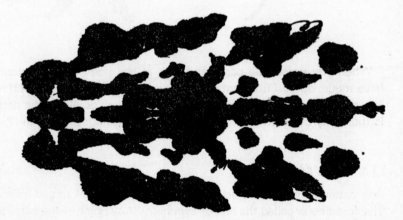

Begin by folding a piece of paper; open it out again and scatter some blots of ink on it. Very big, wet blots will not make good devils so do not use too much! Fold the paper again on the same line as before; the ink will then spread out between the two layers of paper. When it is opened out again you will be able to see the pattern your blots have made.

These blots   made   this pattern.

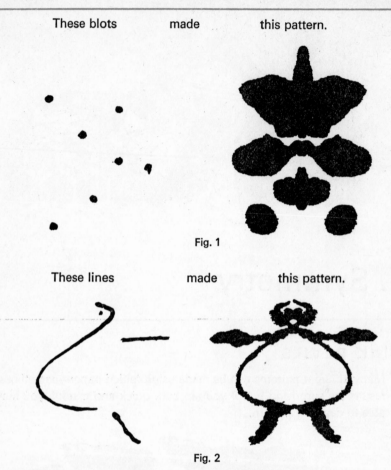

Fig. 1

These lines   made   this pattern.

Fig. 2

When you unfold the paper and look at any point of the pattern you have made, do you find that this point is the same distance from the fold line as the smudge it has made? Is this true of all points on the pattern? Is there any other line which divides the pattern equally like this?

2. LINE SYMMETRY

Any patterns like the ink-devils are called symmetrical (equal measure). The fold line is called the line of symmetry. Any point of the pattern will have its counterpart an equal distance on the opposite side of this line.

Exercise A

In Questions 1–5, the line of symmetry and half of the pattern have been drawn; copy them and complete the patterns.

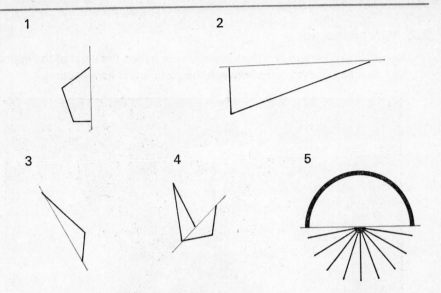

1   2

3   4   5

Work in pairs. One of you draw half a pattern as in Questions 1–5 and allow your neighbour to complete it.

Questions 6–10 show complete patterns. Copy them and draw in the line of symmetry in colour.

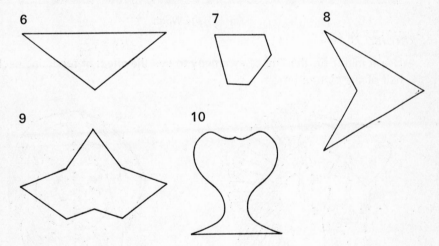

6   7   8

9   10

2.1 Ideas for everyone

Make a classroom display using:

(*a*) the best ink devils arranged with their lines of symmetry pointing in different directions;

(*b*) symmetrical parts of advertisements cut from magazines or newspapers. The brightly coloured ones are best.

2.2 Mirror magic

If you place a picture or a drawing against a mirror, the edge of the mirror acts as a line of symmetry between the picture and its reflection.

Fig. 3. Harry Worth

Exercise B

Use a mirror on the line of symmetry to see the effect of repeating each half of the picture.

1   2

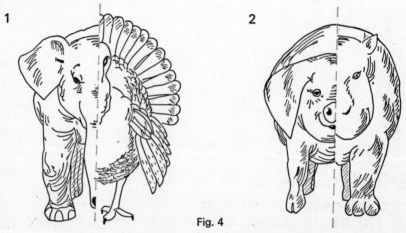

Fig. 4

3   Draw half-and-half objects as illustrated and use the mirror to complete them.

2.3 More ideas for everyone

1   Collect as many different leaves as you can and press them between two pieces of paper weighted by heavy books. When they are really flat, find their lines of symmetry. Arrange and stick them on a large sheet of paper with the lines of symmetry marked in colour.

2   Make drawings or collect pictures of buildings or other man-made objects which show a clear line of symmetry.

Exercise C

You will need lots of paper to do this. Thin paper is cheaper and works very well.

1   Fold a piece of paper once (look at Figure 5), then cut off a corner.

(*a*) Write down the name of the shape you expect to cut off.
(*b*) Open out the piece you have cut off and write down the name of the shape you actually did get.
(*c*) What can you say about the sides and angles of this figure?
(*d*) What line does the fold represent?
(*e*) What can you say about the two parts of the figure on either side of the fold?
(*f*)   Draw a diagram to show how you would cut the paper so that one of the angles of the figure would be a right-angle.

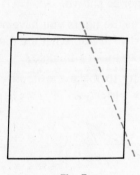

Fig. 5

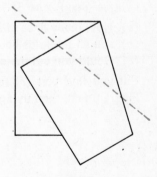

Fig. 6

2   Fold the paper once with an oblique fold (see Figure 6) and cut across the corner.
   Write down:
(*a*) the name of the shape you expected to get;
(*b*) the name of the shape you do get.

3   Do the same as for Question 2 but make the oblique fold at a different angle. Answer the same two questions.

  In your triangles for Questions 2 and 3 what does the fold line represent?

4   Fold a piece of paper in four as shown in Figure 7. Cut across the corner.

(a) What sort of shape did you expect to see this time?
(b) What shape have you actually got?
(c) What lines do the folds represent?
(d) Draw a diagram to show how you would make the cut so that the shape you got would be a square. Do the folds give all the lines of symmetry?

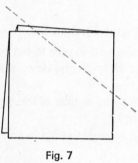

Fig. 7

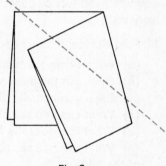

Fig. 8

5   Fold your paper in four again but this time with the second fold oblique (see Figure 8). Cut the corner as shown.

(a) How many lines of symmetry has the figure you have made?
(b) Are all the folds lines of symmetry? If not, what are they?
(c) Could you cut the corner so as to make a triangle?

  If you find part (c) rather hard, try to make the figure shown in Figure 9 first, then try again to make a triangle.

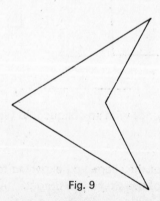

Fig. 9

6   By folding the paper more and more times you can make many different shapes. Try to make the following:

(*a*)   a star (all the folds should go through one point which should be cut out);

(*b*)   a snowflake (this is like a star with six jagged points; cut small pieces out of the fold lines before you unfold it);

(*c*)   a lacy mat.

2.4 Folding without cutting

We have found that we can make four right-angles at a point by folding the paper at that point. In the answers to Exercise C you found that the fold lines halved the angles of your triangles or quadrilaterals (four-sided figures). It is possible to do much more halving by this method and some very interesting results can be found.

When something is divided into two parts in such a way that the two parts are the same, we say that it has been *bisected*.

In Figure 10, *AB* is a line segment. When we say 'the line *AB*' this means an endless straight line through the points *A* and *B*. But when we are only considering points *A* and *B* and the part between them, we refer to 'the line segment *AB*'.

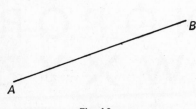

Fig. 10

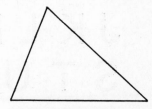

Fig. 11

Has this line segment a line of symmetry? Just looking at it, this does not seem likely and yet it is possible to divide a straight line into two exactly equal parts. Draw a line segment on tracing paper and fold to find the centre. The fold will continue on either side of the centre point. Measure the angles on either side of the fold, between the fold and the line segment *AB*, with a protractor. Can you think of any other lines you could draw to show that this fold is really a line of symmetry?

The triangle shown in Figure 11 is made from three line segments. Use tracing paper or a triangle cut out of plain paper to find the line of symmetry of each of the three sides of the triangle. Do you notice anything about your result?

Symmetry

Exercise D

*(Results are often more clearly shown if lines of
symmetry are drawn in colour)*

1 Draw two triangles which are very different in shape (like those in Figure 12), and find the lines of symmetry for each of the sides of each triangle. Do these lines of symmetry intersect at one point? Is this point inside or outside the triangle?

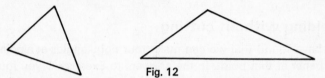

Fig. 12

2 Draw a circle by drawing round a circular object. Find the centre by folding the paper.

3 Copy this set of letters of the alphabet. Try to find lines of symmetry by folding. Remember that not all lines of symmetry are vertical or horizontal and that some shapes may have more than one line of symmetry.

A B C D E F G H I
J K L M N O P Q R
S T U V W X Y Z

4 Find as many lines of symmetry as you can for each of the following figures. Copy them and sketch in the lines.

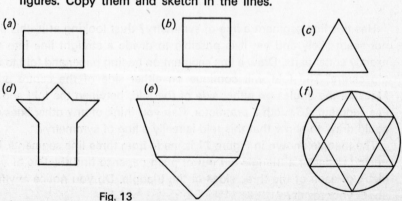

Fig. 13

76

2.5 More about bisecting

In Section 2.4 we learnt about bisecting line segments. The fold line, or line of symmetry, is called the *mediator* of the line segment. The line which cuts an angle into two exactly equal parts is called an *angle bisector*.

For this next exercise you will need pinboard or squared paper.

Exercise E

1   Join the points (3, 1) and (3, 5). Draw in the mediator of this line segment. What is its equation?

2   Draw the line segment joining the points (6, 3) and (2, 3). Draw in the mediator and then write down its equation.

3   Draw the line segment joining the points (1, 1) and (5, 5) and the line segment joining (4, 2) and (1, 5). Is each line the mediator of the other?

4   Draw the two lines $x = 0$ and $y = 0$. Now draw in the bisector of the angle between them. Name three points on this line.

5   Draw two lines that cross (the whole lines in Figure 14), then fold to find both the angle bisectors. (These are shown as broken lines.) Measure the angle between these bisectors. Draw some more pairs of lines and fold to find their angle bisectors. Can you state a fact which you think will apply to all sets of bisectors of this sort?

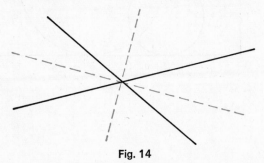

Fig. 14

6   The four corners of a quadrilateral are at the points given by (1, 1), (2, 0), (2, 2), (4, 1). Join these points to form the quadrilateral (it is known as a kite) then draw in any lines of symmetry and state their equations.

7   Copy Figure 15 on page 78. The point (4, 5) is a point at the corner of a figure. The lines $x = 2$ and $y = 4$ are the lines of symmetry of this figure. Find the other corners and then join the points to complete the figure. What is the name of the figure you have drawn?

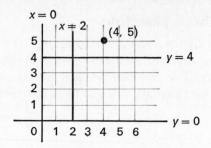

Fig. 15

8   Copy Figure 16. One circle has a radius of 1 centimetre and its centre is the point (2, 1); the centre of the other circle is (4, 2) and its radius 2 centimetres. Draw in the line of symmetry of the figure.

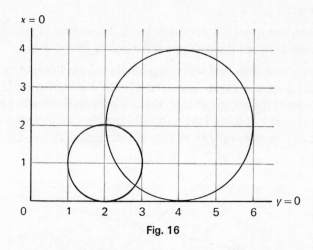

Fig. 16

3. ROTATIONAL SYMMETRY

Trace Figure 17 on two separate pieces of tracing paper. Place one exactly over the other and put a pin through the centres of the figures.

Rotate the top figure until it again covers the lower figure. What fraction of a whole turn has been made?

Again rotate the top figure until it covers the lower figure. What fraction of a turn has been made this time? Is the top figure now in its original position?

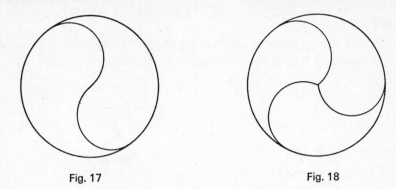

Fig. 17 Fig. 18

Make a tracing of Figure 18 and carry out the experiment just described. What fraction of a turn was made on each occasion before the top figure covered the bottom one? How many thirds of a turn had to be made before the top figure was back in its original position?

Neither of these figures has line symmetry but they both have a sort of regularity discovered by rotation. They are said to have *rotational symmetry*. The point about which these figures have to be rotated to discover this sort of regularity is called the *centre of rotation*. (See page 29.)

Because Figure 17 made two moves before it was back in its original position, it is said to have rotational symmetry of order 2. Figure 18 has rotational symmetry of order 3.

Fig. 19

A figure such as Figure 19 has no rotational symmetry. Copy the figure and choose any point of the plane as a centre of rotation. Could a tracing be rotated about that point so that it falls onto the figure again? Through what part of a turn must it be rotated?

Even figures with no rotational symmetry can be rotated onto themselves by one whole turn. When making tables of the rotational symmetry of different figures, these are given order 1.

Symmetry

Exercise F

1   Use tracing paper to discover the order of rotational symmetry of the following figures about the points marked with red dots.

(a)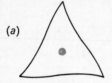

(b)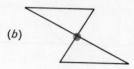

(c)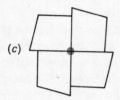

(d)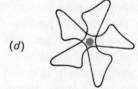

(e)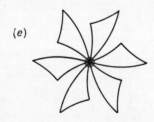

(f)

(g)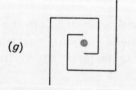

(h)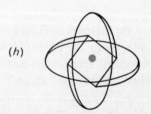

4. LINE AND ROTATIONAL SYMMETRY

Figure 20 (*a*) has rotational symmetry of order 4. But it also has line symmetry. How many lines of symmetry has it? What is the angle between each line of symmetry and the next?

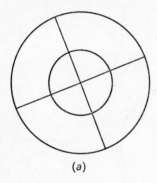 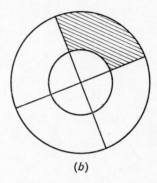

(*a*)   (*b*)

Fig. 20

In Figure 20 (*b*), a section has been shaded. Think of the shading as having changed the figure. This figure has no rotational symmetry and it has only one line of symmetry. Make a copy and shade another section to obtain a new figure with two lines of symmetry and rotational symmetry of order 2. Shade a third section so that the figure again only has one line of symmetry and loses its rotational symmetry. Can you shade a fourth section to give rotational symmetry of order 2? How many lines of symmetry has it now?

Exercise G

1   Trace this pattern. On your tracing draw as many lines of symmetry as you can find. Does this pattern have rotational symmetry about its centre? If so, of what order is it?

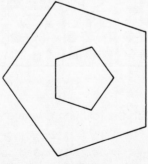

Fig. 21

2 List the symmetries of the following figures. Show your results in a table like this:

Figure	Lines of symmetry	Order of rotational symmetry
a	0	2
b		
c		
d		
e		
f		

(a)

(b)

(c)

(d)

(e)

(f)

Fig. 22

3 List the symmetries of the eight diagrams in Figure 23 as in Question 2.

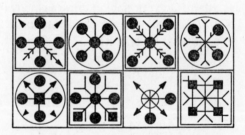

Fig. 23

4 Design patterns with the following symmetries:

	a	b	c	d	e	f	g
Number of lines	4	1	3	2	0	1	6
Order of rotation	4	1	3	2	5	2	6

5 List the symmetries of the following figures. State whether any of the lines of symmetry are mediators or angle bisectors or both:

(a) square;   (b) rectangle (which is not a square);
(c) parallelogram (which is not a rectangle);
(d) equilateral triangle;
(e) isosceles triangle which is not equilateral.

6 Here are some of the patterns seen during a performance by a Formation Dancing Team. Give the symmetries of these patterns thinking of

(a) couples as a unit (one black spot, one red spot);
(b) each person (black spots and red spots) separately.

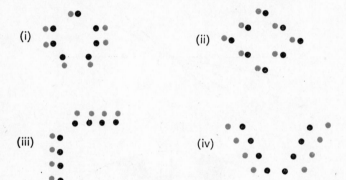

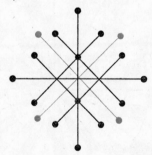

7 Here is a design for a piece of costume jewellery. Discuss its symmetries.

8 Design a piece of costume jewellery to be used as a brooch or a pendant.

9 Design an ornamental star for the top of a Christmas tree.

Interlude

MAKING PATTERNS

Equipment: plain paper; protractor; compasses; ruler. Mark a point near the centre of your paper. Draw straight lines which make angles of 10° with each other at this point. Here are the first five:

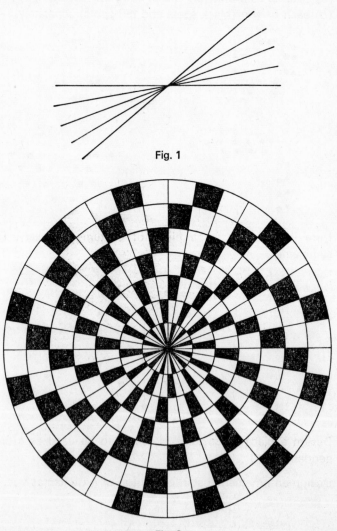

Fig. 1

Fig. 2

Using this point as centre, draw circles of radii 1 cm, 2 cm, 3 cm, 4 cm, 5 cm, etc.

Colour the drawing to make many different patterns. Two shown here have a 'spiral' effect (see Figures 2 and 3). Design some 'spiral' patterns of your own. Figure 4 shows another effect that can be achieved.

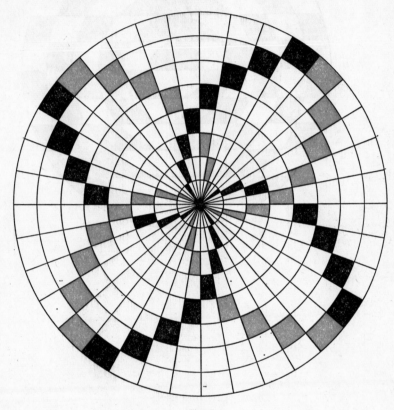

Fig. 3

Fig. 4

Revision exercises

Quick quiz, no. 1

1 $11 \times 12 = ?$

2 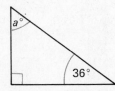 Find a.

3 Which of these are rectangle numbers? 14, 72, 1, 11, 2, 9, 5.

4 $100_{five} \times 14_{five} = ?$

5 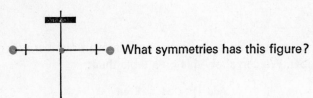 What symmetries has this figure?

6 Three corners of a square have coordinates (0, 0), (0, 1) and (1, 1) respectively. Give the coordinates of the fourth corner.

Quick quiz, no. 2

1 15°, 100°, 340°, 72°, 69°, 89°. Which of these angles are acute?

2 Write down the first four multiples of 13.

3 $140_{five} + 401_{five} = ?$

4 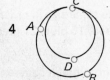 Through how many turns would you rotate in walking round this path in the order $ABCDCA$?

5 How many lines of symmetry has a rectangle?

6 What are the missing numbers? 121, 100, —, 64, —, 36, —, —.

Revision exercises

Exercise A

1 (a) Join each point to the next; (1, 0), (3, 5), (5, 0), ($\frac{1}{2}$, 3), (5$\frac{1}{2}$, 3), (1, 0). How many lines of symmetry has the figure?

(b) Describe this Christmas tree by its coordinates.

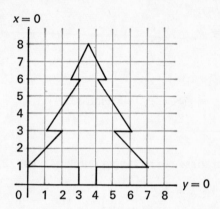

2 (a) When you add an odd number and an even number you get an odd number. We can show this on a table thus:

Add	Odd	Even
Odd	—	Odd
Even	—	—

Copy and fill in the rest of the table.

(b) Now make a multiplication table for odd and even numbers. One entry is filled in.

Multiply	Odd	Even
Odd	—	—
Even	—	Even

3 Some schoolgirls have knitted 100 squares of the same size in order to make a refugee blanket. 30 of these squares are red, 15 blue, 21 green, 23 yellow and the rest are mauve.

(a) What fraction of the blanket will be made from green squares?

(b) What fraction of the blanket will be made from mauve squares?

(c) What fraction of the blanket will be made from red and blue squares?

4   A mysterious race in the Amazonian jungle calculates that

$$21 + 14 = 40.$$

How many fingers do you think they are likely to have?

5   Calculate the size of the lettered angles in degrees.

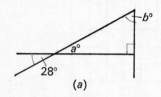 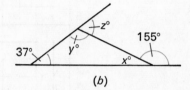

(a)   (b)

Exercise B

1   When a turkey weighing 10 kg is placed on a butcher's weighing machine, the pointer on the dial turns through 180°. Through how many degrees will the pointer turn when weighing 0·5 kg of steak?
   Another customer buys a joint of lamb and this time the pointer rotates through 45°. How much did this joint weigh?

2   The line $x = 3$ is a line of symmetry of a quadrilateral. Two of the vertices are (2, 3) and (4, 1).
   Write down the coordinates of the other two vertices.
   How many lines of symmetry has the completed figure? What are the coordinates of the point about which the figure has rotational symmetry of order 4?

3   Since spiders have eight legs, we could assume that intelligent spiders would use an arithmetic to the base eight! If flies cost 3_{eight} pence each, bees cost 12_{eight} pence each, find the cost of 6 flies and 4 bees in spiders' pence.

4   If $AC = 10$ cm, draw the following figure accurately. Measure *CD*.

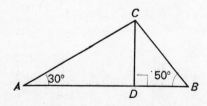

5   How do you get to the centre of this maze? Give your path by stating
    the coordinates of the squares where you turn.

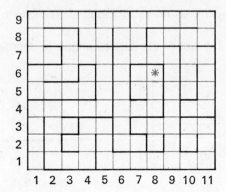

6. A quick look at fractions

1. PARTS OF A WHOLE

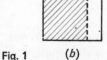

(a)   Fig. 1   (b)

Look at these two squares. Each has been split into two parts (shaded and unshaded), but not in the same way. What is the difference between them? In Figure 1 (a) either part is *one-half* of the square, but is this true in Figure 1 (b)?

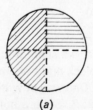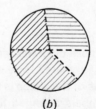

(a)   Fig. 2   (b)

Next look at these two circles. Each has been split into four parts. Is there a difference in the way they have been split? In Figure 2 (a) we could choose any part and say that we had *one-quarter* of the circle. Could we do the same in Figure 2 (b)?

Fractions

Exercise A

1 Which of the following figures have been split into parts of the same size?

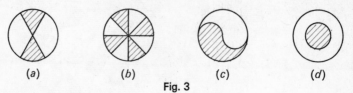

(a)   (b)   (c)   (d)

Fig. 3

2 Split each of these figures into the required number of parts of the same shape and size *by eye*.

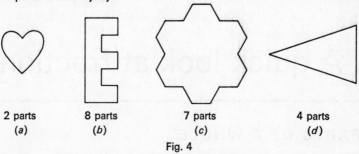

2 parts   8 parts   7 parts   4 parts
(a)   (b)   (c)   (d)

Fig. 4

3 'Peter's got the bigger half', shouted Paul. What is wrong with this remark?

Sometimes it is possible to split a shape into a given number of parts, each of the same size in more than one way. Figure 5 shows three different ways of splitting a disc into 6 equal parts.

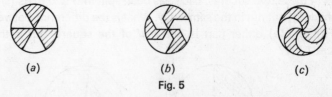

(a)   (b)   (c)

Fig. 5

In any of these diagrams, each part is a sixth of the whole. How many white sixths are there? How many black and how many red sixths?

'Two-sixths of the shape is black.' One way of writing 'two-sixths' is to use two numbers arranged like this: $\frac{2}{6}$. Such a number pair is called a 'fraction'.

The bottom number of a fraction tells us the number of parts into which the shape has been split. (Zero can never be the bottom number of a fraction because it is impossible for one whole to be made from no parts!) The top number indicates how many of these parts we are referring to.

Example 1

In Figure 5, each red shaded part represents *one-sixth* ($\frac{1}{6}$) of the disc.

Example 2

This disc is split into 8 equal parts, with 3 of them shaded. We say that *three-eighths* ($\frac{3}{8}$) of the disc is shaded.

Example 3

This square is divided into 12 equal parts with 7 of them shaded. We say that *seven-twelfths* ($\frac{7}{12}$) of the square is shaded.

Example 4

This disc has not been split into parts. The whole is the only part so that 1 whole disc ($\frac{1}{1}$) is shaded.

Exercise B

1 Write each of the following as a fraction:
   (*a*) one-half;   (*b*) two-thirds;
   (*c*) five-twelfths;   (*d*) eight-ninths.

2 Write down each fraction in words:
   (*a*) $\frac{2}{5}$;   (*b*) $\frac{3}{4}$;   (*c*) $\frac{7}{10}$;   (*d*) $\frac{11}{12}$.

3 What fraction of each figure is shaded?

(*a*)

(*b*)

(*c*)

(*d*)

(*e*)   Fig. 6

(*f*)

93

4 Trace each figure and shade the fraction indicated. (Remember that first you must split it into parts of equal shape and size.)

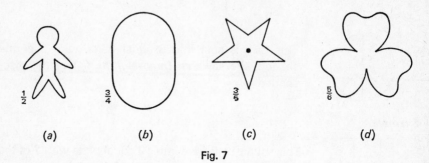

(a)   (b)   (c)   (d)

Fig. 7

5 (a) What is one-tenth of a centimetre called?
   (b) What is one-sixtieth of an hour called?
   (c) What is one-seventh of a week called?
   (d) What is one-hundredth of a pound (£) called?

The same piece of an object may be described by 'different looking' fractions. Here each fraction gives one-half of the disc.

Fig. 8

Exercise C

1 How much of each figure is shaded? Give as many 'different looking' fractions as you can in each case.

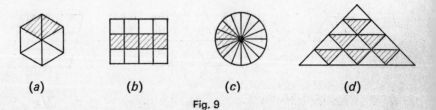

(a)   (b)   (c)   (d)

Fig. 9

2. MIXED NUMBERS

Example 5

These seven quarters ($\frac{7}{4}$) of a disc together form one and three-quarters ($1\frac{3}{4}$) discs.

We can write: $\frac{7}{4} = 1\frac{3}{4}$.

Example 6

These eight quarters ($\frac{8}{4}$) of a disc together form two whole (2) discs.

We write: $\frac{8}{4} = 2$.

How do the fractions $\frac{7}{4}$ and $\frac{8}{4}$ differ from the fractions you have met so far in this chapter? Any fraction greater than one is equal *either* to a *'mixed number'* (as in Example 5) *or* a *'whole number'* (as in Example 6).

Example 7

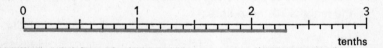

The figure shows a line marked in units and tenths of one unit. We can give the length of the red line as:

   (i) a fraction greater than one (that is, $\frac{23}{10}$ of a unit), or
  (ii) a mixed number (that is $2\frac{3}{10}$ units).

Fractions

Exercise D

1 Write down the connection between fractions and mixed numbers illustrated by each of the following diagrams:

(a)  give

(b)  give

(c) 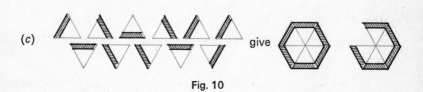 give

Fig. 10

2 Give each length as a fraction greater than one, and then as a mixed or a whole number.

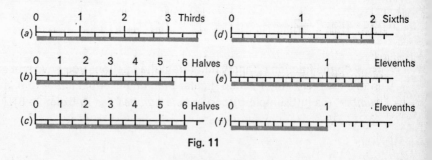

Fig. 11

3 Use the side of an 'old' ruler marked in eighths of an inch to measure the lengths of these lines:

(a) ＿＿＿＿＿＿＿   (c) ＿＿＿＿＿＿＿＿＿＿＿＿＿

(b) ＿＿＿＿＿＿＿＿＿＿   (d) ＿＿＿＿＿＿＿＿＿＿＿

Fig. 12

Give the length of each line in two ways (as in Question 2).

4   Is each fraction less than one, equal to one, or greater than one?

(a) $\frac{3}{4}$;   (b) $\frac{99}{100}$;   (c) $\frac{100}{100}$;   (d) $\frac{21}{20}$;

(e) $\frac{100}{3}$;   (f) $\frac{20}{33}$;   (g) $\frac{15}{5}$;   (h) $\frac{127}{127}$;

(i) $\frac{1001}{1000}$.

3. FRACTIONS WITH THE SAME BOTTOM NUMBER

Fractions with the same bottom number are easy to compare in size. These fractions: $\frac{3}{7}, \frac{5}{7}, \frac{7}{7}, \frac{13}{7}, \frac{22}{7}, \frac{28}{7}$ could all be shown on a number line, marked out in sevenths:

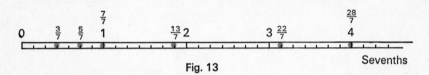

Fig. 13   Sevenths

This shows them in order of size. Numbers to the left are smaller than numbers to the right.

You should now be able to arrange the following fractions in order of size without first marking them on a number line:

$$\frac{2}{9}, \quad \frac{7}{9}, \quad \frac{22}{9}, \quad \frac{4}{9}, \quad \frac{15}{9}.$$

How did you do this?

Fractions with the same bottom number are also easy to add together. This is because we are dealing with parts of the same size. It is not so easy to add together fractions with different bottom numbers. This should be clear if you look at the following diagrams.

Example 8

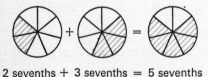

2 sevenths + 3 sevenths = 5 sevenths

Fig. 14 (*a*)

Example 9

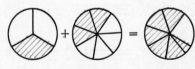

1 third + 3 sevenths = ___ ?

Fig. 14 (*b*)

(You will learn to do the addition of Example 9 later.)

The same thing is true if you want to take one fraction away from another.

Fractions

Example 10

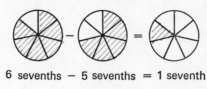

6 sevenths − 5 sevenths = 1 seventh

Fig. 15

Examples 8 and 10 could also have been shown on a number line marked out in sevenths:

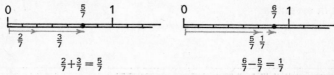

$\frac{2}{7}+\frac{3}{7}=\frac{5}{7}$ $\frac{6}{7}-\frac{5}{7}=\frac{1}{7}$

Fig. 16

Exercise E

1   Arrange the following fractions in order of size (smallest first):

$$\frac{13}{13}, \quad \frac{1}{13}, \quad \frac{15}{13}, \quad \frac{6}{13}, \quad \frac{20}{13}, \quad \frac{0}{13}.$$

2   The sign '<' means 'is less than', and the sign '>' means 'is greater than'.

Which of the following statements are true and which are false?

(a) 3 quarters > 1 quarter;   (b) 4 halves < 1 half;
(c) 5 tenths < 11 tenths;   (d) $\frac{5}{7} < \frac{8}{7}$;
(e) $\frac{4}{3} < \frac{7}{3}$;   (f) $\frac{15}{5} > \frac{3}{5}$.

3   Give the addition or subtraction shown on each line.

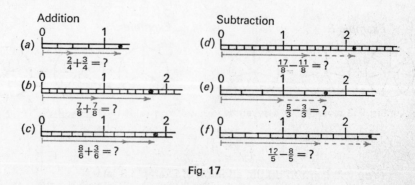

Fig. 17

When can you give your answer as a mixed number?

4 Calculate:

(a) 3 fifths + 1 fifth;   (b) 3 sevenths + 5 sevenths;

(c) 17 hundredths − 9 hundredths;

(d) $\frac{5}{9} - \frac{2}{9}$;   (e) $\frac{14}{5} + \frac{3}{5}$;   (f) $\frac{1}{2} + \frac{1}{2}$;

(g) $\frac{2}{3} - \frac{2}{3}$;   (h) $\frac{1001}{1005} + \frac{4}{1005}$;   (i) $\frac{11}{7} - \frac{9}{7}$.

Exercise F (Miscellaneous)

1 The points marked in red represent fractions greater than one. Give them as mixed or whole numbers.

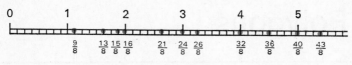

Fig. 18

2 Belinda had an orange consisting of 12 equal pieces.

(a) She ate 5 of these pieces. What fraction of the orange had she eaten?

(b) Her brother ate 4 of them. How much had he eaten?

(c) What fraction of the orange was left?

3 Complete the following:

(a) $1 = \frac{?}{8}$;   (b) $2 = \frac{?}{8}$;   (c) $3 = \frac{?}{8}$;

(d) $3 = \frac{?}{2}$;   (e) $10 = \frac{?}{3}$;   (f) $4 = \frac{?}{5}$;

(g) $1\frac{1}{2} = \frac{?}{2}$;   (h) $1\frac{3}{5} = \frac{?}{5}$;   (i) $2\frac{3}{4} = \frac{?}{4}$.

4 Change each mixed number to a fraction greater than one. (Use the side of an 'old' ruler marked in eighths of an inch to help you if necessary.)

(a) $1\frac{1}{8}$;   (b) $1\frac{3}{8}$;   (c) $1\frac{7}{8}$;

(d) $2\frac{3}{8}$;   (e) $3\frac{5}{8}$;   (f) $5\frac{7}{8}$.

5 Change each of these fractions to either a mixed number or a whole number. (Use the side of your ruler marked in tenths of a centimetre to help you if necessary.)

(a) $\frac{11}{10}$;   (b) $\frac{20}{10}$;   (c) $\frac{17}{10}$;

(d) $\frac{40}{10}$;   (e) $\frac{23}{10}$;   (f) $\frac{55}{10}$.

6 Al, Joe, Nancy and Sam have just dug up a treasure. Joe and Nancy each want $\frac{3}{10}$ of the money while Sam wants $\frac{5}{10}$ of it. Why is this impossible? Al persuades Joe and Nancy to accept $\frac{3}{13}$ each and Sam to accept $\frac{5}{13}$. How much is left for him? Do you think he was wise?

7. Polygons

1. NAMING POLYGONS

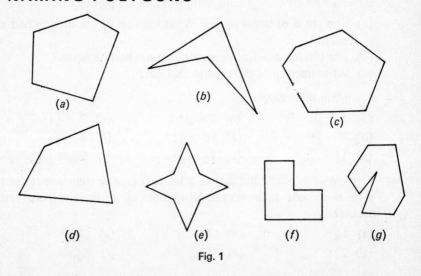

Fig. 1

The plane shapes in Figure 1 are all *polygons*. We use the word 'plane' when the shapes lie in a flat surface, such as the top of a polished table.

The boundary of a polygon is formed from parts (or segments) of straight lines. These line segments are called the *sides* or *edges* of the polygon.

The names of some of the more common polygons are:

Triangle   (3 sides)   Triangle means three angles
Quadrilateral   (4 sides)   Quadrilateral means four sides
Pentagon   (5 sides)   Pentagon means five corners

Hexagon (6 sides) Hexagon means six corners
Octagon (8 sides) Octagon means eight corners

(*a*) Name each of the polygons in Figure 1.

(*b*)

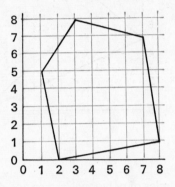

Fig. 2

Copy and name the polygon shown in Figure 2.

A and *B* are *any* two points of the polygon. In Figure 3, *AB* lies entirely within the polygon. Can you find *A* and *B* so that part of the line segment *AB* lies outside the polygon?

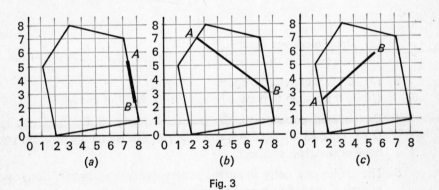

(*a*)   (*b*)   (*c*)

Fig. 3

(*c*) Copy and name the polygon shown in Figure 4. Can you find two points *A* and *B* of the polygon so that *AB* lies partly outside the polygon?

If, for every pair of points of the polygon, the line segment joining them lies entirely within the polygon, then the polygon is said to be *convex*.

The pentagon in Figure 2 is convex; the quadrilateral in Figure 4 is not convex.

(*d*) Look at Figure 1. Which of these polygons are convex?

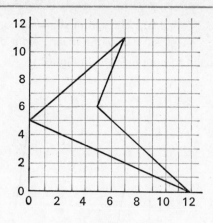

Fig. 4

Exercise A

1 Give five examples of polygonal frames and draw diagrams to illustrate them. For example, the bicycle frame shown in Figure 5.

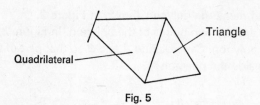

Quadrilateral —

Triangle

Fig. 5

2 (*a*) Draw a convex triangle.
  (*b*) Is it possible to draw a triangle which is not convex?

3 (*a*) Draw a convex hexagon.
  (*b*) Is it possible to draw a hexagon which is not convex?

4 On squared paper, mark the points A (1, 1), B (2, 5), C (4, 4), D (5, 1), E (3, 2). Join AB, BC, CD, DE, EA. Name the polygon you have drawn. Is it convex?

5 The angles of a polygon are the angles *inside* the polygon. Copy and complete the following table for the polygons in Figure 1.

Figure	Number of reflex angles	Convex yes or no
a	0	Yes
b	1	No
c		
d		
e		
f		
g		

Can you draw a convex polygon which has a reflex angle?

6 Draw, if possible, a pentagon which has:

(a) no reflex angles;   (b) one reflex angle;

(c) two reflex angles;   (d) three reflex angles.

7 How many angles has a hexagon?
   Sketch, if possible, hexagons which have

(a) one right-angle;   (b) two right-angles;

(c) three right-angles;   (d) four right-angles;

(e) five right-angles;   (f) six right-angles.

2. ANGLES OF POLYGONS

(a) Sketch a convex pentagon like the one in Figure 6. A point where two sides meet is called a *vertex*. Draw lines from A to all the other vertices except B and E. These are the *diagonals* from A. Why are AB and AE not called diagonals?

How many diagonals from A can you draw? Into how many cells is the pentagon divided? What shape are these cells?

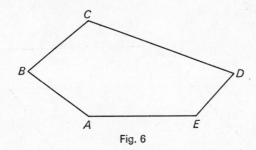

Fig. 6

(b) Copy and complete the following table.

Convex polygon	Number of diagonals from one vertex	Number of cells	Shape of each cell
Quadrilateral			
Pentagon	2	3	Triangular
Hexagon			
Octagon			

(c) The pentagon is divided into 3 triangular cells (see Figure 7). Do the angles of the 3 triangles make up the angles of the pentagon? What is the sum of the angles of a triangle? What is the sum of the angles of the pentagon?

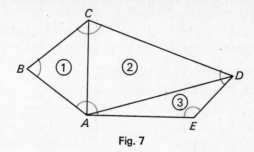

Fig. 7

(*d*) Draw a convex hexagon. Draw all the diagonals through one of the vertices. How many triangular cells are there? What is the sum of the angles of the hexagon?

(*e*) Use the method of (*c*) and (*d*) to find the sum of the angles of a convex octagon.

Experiment 1

Equipment: chalk or rope, a blackboard protractor.

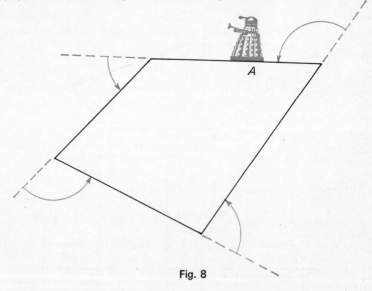

Fig. 8

Using chalk (or rope) mark out a large convex quadrilateral on the playground (or classroom floor). Start at *A* and walk once round the boundary of the quadrilateral turning always to the left. Ask a friend to measure the angle through which you turn at each vertex. What is the sum of these angles? Record your result.

Repeat this experiment for other convex polygons.

What happens when the polygon is not convex?

Experiment 2

Equipment: scissors, gummed paper.

Draw a convex quadrilateral on the gummed paper and cut it out. Mark the angles of the quadrilateral and tear off each corner. Place the four corners of the quadrilateral together (see Figure 10) and stick them into your exercise book.

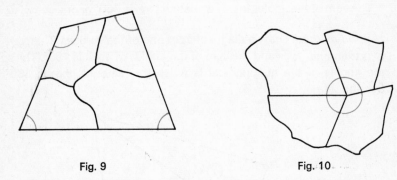

Fig. 9   Fig. 10

What can you say about the angles of your quadrilateral? Does your result depend upon the shape of the quadrilateral which you draw?

Example 1

Find the sum of the angles of the convex quadrilateral in Figure 11. All angle measurements are in degrees.

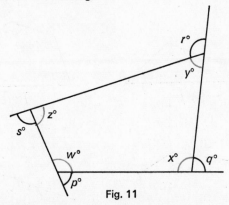

Fig. 11

First method. Imagine that you walk along the boundary of the quadrilateral. When you return to the starting point you have rotated through one complete turn.

At each corner you turn through the black angle; the four black angles together form one whole turn or 360°.

105

Each black angle together with its red angle adds up to 180°.

4 black angles+4 red angles = $4 \times 180° = 720°$

4 red angles = $720° - 4$ black angles

$= 720° - 360°$

$= 360°.$

The sum of the angles inside a quadrilateral is 360° or one complete turn.

Second method. Draw a diagonal from one of the vertices. There are now two triangular cells and the sum of the angles of each is 180°. The sum of the angles of the quadrilateral is twice this amount, that is 360° (see Section 2 (c)).

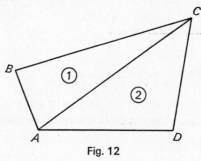

Fig. 12

Exercise B

1   Find the angles represented by small letters in Figure 13.

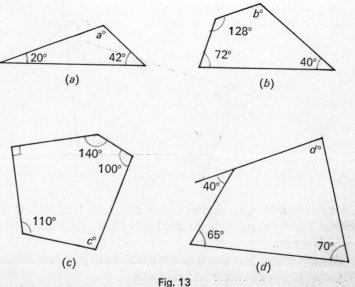

Fig. 13

2   Draw a quadrilateral with a reflex angle. This is called a 're-entrant' quadrilateral. Is the sum of the angles still 360°?

3   Three angles of a quadrilateral are each 100°. What size is the fourth angle?

4   Name the polygons in Figure 14 and find the sum of their angles. (Be careful to use the angles which are *inside* the polygons. Do not use a protractor.)

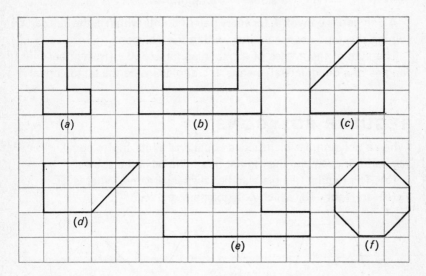

Fig. 14

5   Use the first method of Example 1 to find the sum of the angles of a convex pentagon.

6   Four angles of a pentagon are each 110°. What size is the fifth angle?

7   Find the sum of the angles of a seven-sided polygon (a heptagon).

8   Find the sum of the angles of a twelve-sided figure (a dodecagon).

9   Is it possible to draw a polygon with angles which add up to (*a*) 450°; (*b*) 900°?

10   The angles of a polygon add up to 360°. Must the polygon be a quadrilateral?

11   The angles of a polygon add up to 1080°; how many sides has it? How many vertices has it?

SUMMARY

A polygon is a plane figure with straight sides.
Here are the names of some important ones:

3 sides	triangle;
4 sides	quadrilateral;
5 sides	pentagon;
6 sides	hexagon;
8 sides	octagon.

A polygon is convex if, for every pair of points within it, the line segment joining those points lies entirely within the polygon.

The sum of the angles of a quadrilateral is 360°. (Remember that the 'angles of a quadrilateral' means 'the angles inside the quadrilateral'.)

3. REGULAR POLYGONS

When a polygon has all its sides equal *and* all its angles equal, it is called *regular*. For example, the regular quadrilateral is the square.

(a) The regular triangle also has a special name. What is it?

(b) In Figure 15, which polygons are regular?

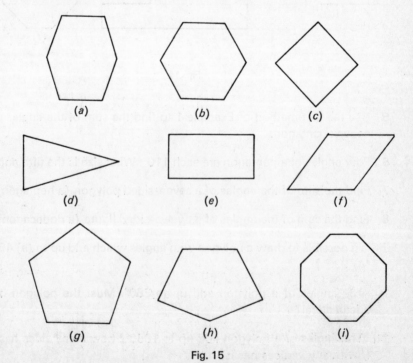

Fig. 15

(c) Comment on the symmetries of these polygons.

(d) What is the sum of the angles of a regular quadrilateral? Work out the number of degrees in each angle.

(e) How many degrees are there in each angle of a regular triangle?

(f) When a polygon is regular it fits exactly into a circle. Figure 16 shows a regular pentagon fitting exactly into a circle with centre O. How many degrees are there in ∠BOC, ∠COD, ∠DOE, ∠EOA, and ∠AOB?

Exercise C

1   In Figure 16, O is the centre of the circle. Find ∠BOC.
    What kind of triangle is BOC?
    What are the sizes of ∠OBC, ∠OCB and ∠OBA?
    How many degrees are there in an angle of a regular pentagon?

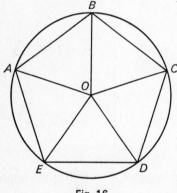
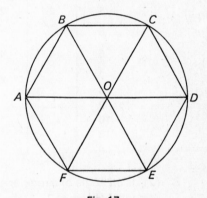

Fig. 16   Fig. 17

2   Look at Figure 16. What is the size of each of the angles at the centre O?
    By starting with a circle of radius 6 cm, make an accurate drawing of a regular pentagon.

3   In Figure 17, ABCDEF is a regular hexagon in a circle whose centre is O. Find the size of ∠AOF.
    What kind of triangle is AOF?
    Find the sizes of ∠OAF, ∠OFA and ∠OFE.
    How many degrees are there in an angle of a regular hexagon?

4   Look at Figure 17. The regular hexagon is divided into six triangles. What kind of triangles are they? By starting with a circle of radius 5 cm, make an accurate drawing of a regular hexagon.
    Can you draw a regular hexagon without using a protractor?

5 Draw a large regular pentagon by first drawing a circle. Draw all the diagonals and you will find a smaller regular pentagon inside the first one. Draw the diagonals of the smaller pentagon and repeat the process as many times as you can.

6 How many degrees are there in an angle of a regular octagon?

7 Copy and complete the following table about convex polygons. The 'number of triangles' is the number which are formed when all the diagonals are drawn from *one* vertex.

Number of sides	Number of triangles	Sum of all angles	Angle of regular polygon
3	1	180°	$\dfrac{180°}{3} = 60°$
4	2	$2 \times 180° = 360°$	$\dfrac{360°}{4} = 90°$
5			
6	4	$4 \times 180° = 720°$	$\dfrac{720°}{6} = 120°$
7			
8			
9			
10			
12			
n			

8 (*a*) Is an angle of a regular octagon larger or smaller than the angle of a regular pentagon?
(*b*) Is an angle of a regular 40-sided polygon larger or smaller than the angle of a regular 20-sided polygon?

D 9 (*a*) What is the smallest possible angle of a regular polygon? Which regular polygon has angles of this size?
(*b*) What is the smallest angle which is too big to be an angle of a regular polygon?

10 Is it possible for the angle of a regular polygon to be: (*a*) 90°; (*b*) 75°; (*c*) 108°? Give reasons for your answers.

11 The angle of a regular polygon is 162°. How many sides has it?
(*Hint*: find what angle you would turn through at each vertex in walking round it.)

12 Take a strip of paper about 25 cm long and 2·5 cm wide. Tie a knot in it (see Figure 18*a*) and pull it tight (see Figure 18*b*).

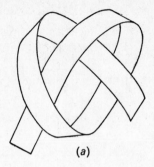

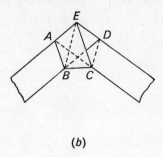

(a)   (b)

Fig. 18

Flatten your knot very carefully.

What shape is *ABCDE*?

Can you obtain any other regular polygons by folding paper? How?

13 Fit pennies together flat on a table so that one is surrounded by a ring made of the others. How many pennies are there altogether? What shape is obtained by joining with straight lines the centres of the pennies of the outer ring?

SUMMARY

A regular polygon has all its sides equal *and* all its angles equal.

A regular polygon fits exactly into a circle (that is, a circle can be drawn to pass through all the vertices of the polygon).

A regular triangle is an equilateral triangle.

A regular quadrilateral is a square.

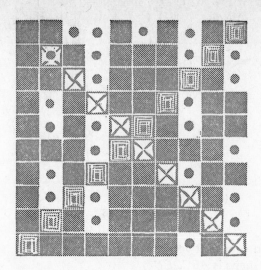

8. Further number patterns

1. MULTIPLES AND COMMON MULTIPLES

The following numbers have all been expressed in terms of two of their factors:

$$6 = 2 \times 3 \qquad 12 = 4 \times 3 \qquad 18 = 6 \times 3$$

$$9 = 3 \times 3 \qquad 15 = 5 \times 3 \qquad 21 = 7 \times 3$$

Each of these numbers has 3 as one of its factors and so we say that these rectangle numbers are all *multiples* of 3. They are a few of the members of the set of multiples of 3.

$$\{\text{multiples of } 3\} = \{3, 6, 9, 12, 15, 18, 21, 24, \ldots\}.$$

This set is not like the others you have met because there are many more multiples of three than we have shown. In fact we can go on multiplying numbers by three for as long as we like, and you will always get new numbers that are members of the set.

In the same way:

$$\{\text{multiples of } 7\} = \{7, 14, 21, 28, 35, 42, \ldots\}.$$

1.1 Multiple patterns

Rule out a square with eleven spaces across and eleven spaces down. Number the top and left-hand edges as in the diagram. This shows the units and the tens digits for the numbers.

Units digits

	0	1	2	3	4	5	6	7	8	9
0										
1										
2										
3										
4										
5										
6										
7										
8										
9										

Tens digits

Put a 2 (or some 2-mark, for example, a coloured dot) in the space for 2 and in every second space. This marks the multiples of 2.

Put a 3 (or some 3-mark) in the space for 3 and in every third space.

Put a 4 (or a 4-mark) in the space for 4 and in every fourth space. As $4 = 2 \times 2$, make the 4-mark a repeated 2-mark. As $6 = 2 \times 3$, you will find a 2-mark and a 3-mark in the space for 6. So let this pair form the 6-mark.

Continue at least as far as multiples of 11. Invent new marks for 5, 7 and 11. How are you going to mark 8, 9 and 10? Notice the patterns. Which way do the lines of 3-marks slope? Are the lines of 5-marks across or down the page? Where do the lines of 9-marks cross the lines of 7-marks?

We sometimes use the symbol '∈' to stand for 'is a member of'.

$$27 \in \{\text{multiples of 3}\}$$

is read '27 is a member of the set of multiples of 3'.

Are the following true:

$$14 \in \{\text{multiples of 4}\},$$

$$64 \in \{\text{square numbers}\},$$

$$75 \in \{\text{rectangle numbers}\}?$$

Sometimes numbers are members of several different sets. On your square of multiples, do the sloping lines of 9-marks cross the column of 5-marks? Is it true to say that

$$45 \in \{\text{multiples of 9}\},$$

and that $\qquad 45 \in \{\text{multiples of 5}\}?$

What other numbers can be used instead of 45? These two sets have some members in common; they are said to *intersect*. (See page 25.)

To remind you of the special sign for intersection:

Let *N* stand for the set of multiples of 9 and *F* stand for the multiples of 5. We can write

$$N = \{\text{multiples of } 9\}, \quad F = \{\text{multiples of } 5\}.$$

The intersection of these sets is written $N \cap F$ and this is read '*N* intersection *F*'.

Exercise A

Use the number square to help you to answer these questions. In all the questions, *A*, *B* and *C* refer to the sets defined in Question 1.

1 List the members of the following sets:

$$A = \{\text{multiples of 2 which are less than } 40\},$$

$$B = \{\text{multiples of 3 which are less than } 40\},$$

$$C = \{\text{multiples of 5 which are less than } 40\}.$$

2 Copy the following statements putting in 'is' or 'is not' where you see the space marked —— :

  (*a*) 2 —— a member of *A*;
  (*b*) 20 —— a member of *B*;
  (*c*) 20 —— a member of *C*.

3 Using the symbol ∈, write down the set or sets (*A*, *B* or *C*) to which the following numbers belong. (Notice that $15 \in B$ and $15 \in C$.)

  (*a*) 32; (*b*) 27; (*c*) 28; (*d*) 35; (*e*) 10; (*f*) 18; (*g*) 20;
(*h*) 45; (*i*) 40; (*j*) 36; (*k*) 30; (*l*) 42.

4 Is it true that $20 \in A \cap C$?

5 Find two other members of $A \cap C$.

6 Make a list of all the members of $A \cap B$.

7 List the members of $B \cap C$.

8 Which number is a member of *A*, *B* and *C*, that is of $A \cap B \cap C$?

9 The set $A \cap B$ is the set of numbers less than 40 which are multiples of 2 and 3. This is {common multiples of 2 and 3 which are less than 40}.

Copy and complete the following statement:

$B \cap C = \{$common multiples of ... and ... which are less than...$\}$.

2. PRIME NUMBERS

Prime numbers are very special and important numbers. In a way, they are the 'raw material' from which we make all other numbers. They are like the bricks which go into the building of a house or the paints with which we can make pictures.

Each prime number is bigger than 1 and has only two factors, 1 and itself. So, in a completed table of multiples, any space with just *one* mark must show a prime number.

(To find all the prime numbers up to 100, it might be best to draw a new number square and to use shading rather than number marks. Shade all the multiples of 2 except 2 itself. Look for the next empty square after 2. It is the 3 square. Shade all the multiples of 3 except 3 itself. Look for the next empty square after 3. It is the 5 square. Shade all the multiples of 5 except 5 itself and so on.)

Are there 25 prime numbers less than 100? Is there any regularity in the pattern of numbers between each prime number? Are there the same number of primes numbers between 1 and 50 as between 51 and 100? Would you expect there to be a biggest prime number?

2.1 Prime factors

Example 1

What are the prime factors of 30? Multiply them together.

$$30 = 2 \times 15 \quad \text{but} \quad 15 = 3 \times 5 \quad \text{and so} \quad 30 = 2 \times 3 \times 5.$$

Check with the multiple square and you will see that the square representing 30 has in it the marks for 2, 3 and 5.

$$\{\text{prime factors of } 30\} = \{2, 3, 5\}.$$

Answer the same question about the number 42.

Some of the spaces in our multiple pattern have a mark that is repeated. This shows that we sometimes need to use the same prime factor more than once.

Example 2

Find the prime factors of 12.

$$12 = 2 \times 6 \quad \text{but} \quad 6 = 2 \times 3 \quad \text{and so} \quad 12 = 2 \times 2 \times 3.$$

Although the only distinct prime factors of 12 are 2 and 3 we need to use the 2 twice before we can write down 12 in terms of its prime factors.

Notice that:

(a) {factors of 12} = {1, 2, 3, 4, 6, 12},
(b) {prime factors of 12} = {2, 3},
(c) $12 = 2 \times 2 \times 3$.

115

Example 3

Find the prime factors of 56 and write it as a product of primes.

This number is rather larger than the others we have looked at, so we must think of an orderly way to tackle it. Start by trying to divide it by the smallest prime number. If this divides into it a whole number of times, we know that it is a factor.

$$2)\underline{56}$$
$$2)\underline{28} \quad \text{now try 2 again}$$
$$2)\underline{14} \quad \text{and again}$$
$$\underline{7} \quad \text{and we know that 7 is a prime number.}$$

$$\{\text{prime factors of 56}\} = \{2, 7\},$$

$$56 = 2 \times 2 \times 2 \times 7.$$

In the same way we can show that:

$$36 = 2 \times 2 \times 3 \times 3,$$

$$75 = 3 \times 5 \times 5,$$

$$32 = 2 \times 2 \times 2 \times 2 \times 2.$$

This is a very long way to write out the answers, but we can shorten it.

When you first met square numbers you found that 7×7 could be written as 7^2. We can use the same idea again and write 32 as 2^5 which is read as '2 to the power of 5' or '2 to the fifth'.

In the same way $36 = 2^2 \times 3^2$; $75 = 3 \times 5^2$; and $56 = 2^3 \times 7$.

Exercise B

1 Write each of the following as products of primes:

(a) 8;   (b) 15;   (c) 27;

(d) 54;   (e) 63;   (f) 72.

2.2 Finding prime numbers

Example 4

Is 221 a prime number?

To answer this question we have to find out whether 221 has any prime factors. This is done by dividing by prime numbers to see whether there will be a remainder. Always start with the smallest prime and work your way through.

$\left.\begin{array}{l} 2 \\ 3 \\ 5 \\ 7 \\ 11 \end{array}\right\}$ is not a factor as there is a remainder after dividing 221 by $\left\{\begin{array}{l} 2 \\ 3 \\ 5 \\ 7 \\ 11 \end{array}\right.$

13 is a factor because it divides into 221 exactly 17 times.

So $221 = 13 \times 17$ and is therefore not a prime number.

Exercise C

1 (a) What are the members of the following sets?

$$A = \{\text{factors of } 15\},$$
$$B = \{\text{factors of } 18\},$$
$$C = \{\text{factors of } 12\}.$$

(b) If $P = \{\text{prime numbers}\}$, what are the members of:

$$A \cap P, \quad B \cap P, \quad C \cap P?$$

2 $A = \{\text{prime numbers between} \quad 0 \text{ and } \quad 20\},$
$B = \{\text{prime numbers between } 20 \text{ and } \quad 40\},$
$C = \{\text{prime numbers between } 40 \text{ and } \quad 60\},$
$D = \{\text{prime numbers between } 60 \text{ and } \quad 80\},$
$E = \{\text{prime numbers between } 80 \text{ and } 100\}.$

How many members has each of the sets A, B, C, D and E? From these answers, can you say how many members there would be in the set F if $F = \{\text{prime numbers between } 100 \text{ and } 120\}$? Now find the actual number of primes between 100 and 120. List the members of this set.

3 Find the prime factors of the following numbers, then write them as products of primes:

(a) 20;   (b) 27;   (c) 48;   (d) 231;   (e) 455.

4 Which of the following numbers are prime?

(a) 324;   (b) 927;   (c) 139;   (d) 161;   (e) 199.

5 Write 1000 as a product of primes.

6 Is 2^{10} larger or smaller than 1000? Find the difference.

7 (a) Which number can be written:

$$2^3 \times 3 \times 5^2 \times 11?$$

(b) A different number can be written:

$$2^2 \times 3^2 \times 5 \times 11.$$

Without working out the second number can you say how you know that it will be different?

(*c*) Which of the two numbers is the larger?

8 A quick test to discover if a number is a multiple of 5 is to see if it ends with 5 or 0.

The sum of the digits of a multiple of 3 is also a multiple of 3. For example, we know that 78126 is a multiple of 3 because

$$7+8+1+2+6 = 24 = 3 \times 8.$$

Work out a test which will tell you whether a number is a common multiple of 3 and 5. Which number must also be a factor of such a common multiple? Which of the following numbers is a common multiple of 3 and 5?

(*a*) 3065; (*b*) 8065; (*c*) 4065.

3. TRIANGLE NUMBERS

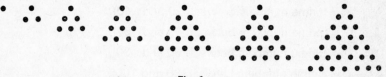

Fig. 1

These patterns of dots give the *triangle numbers*. What triangle numbers are shown? How is each triangle made from the one before? What are the next three triangle numbers? What is the difference between the thirteenth and the twelfth triangle numbers?

We can draw the same triangles in another way. Copy the triangles shown below, then draw two more to show the seventh and eighth triangle numbers.

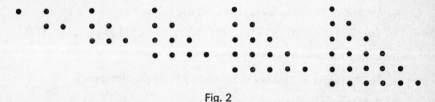

Fig. 2

Look at the patterns in Figure 3. Using both black and red dots we have put two triangle numbers together in each pattern. Does this help you to see a connection between triangle numbers and square numbers?

Fig. 3

Copy Figure 3 and add three more such patterns.

Exercise D

1 What is the sum of:

(*a*) the 2nd and 3rd triangle numbers;

(*b*) the 3rd and 4th triangle numbers;

(*c*) the 4th and 5th triangle numbers;

(*d*) the 10th and 11th triangle numbers?

3.1 Triangle numbers and rectangle numbers

In Figure 4 we have a slightly different pattern of red and black dots. This time we have shown each triangle number twice on the same pattern so that, apart from the first, they make rectangular patterns.

Fig. 4

Which rectangle number is double the third triangle number? The 4th triangle number is $\frac{1}{2}(4 \times 5) = 10$. Write down the 5th, 6th, 7th, 10th and 11th triangle numbers using this method. Do your answers agree with your earlier results?

Can you show that only one of the triangle numbers is a prime number? Which one is it? (If you find this rather hard—have a look at Figure 4.)

Further number patterns

4. ALL SORTS OF NUMBERS
Exercise E

In Questions 1 and 2 the letters *P*, *R*, *S* and *T* stand for the sets

P = {prime numbers less than 40},
R = {rectangle numbers less than 40},
S = {square numbers less than 40},
T = {triangle numbers less than 40}.

1 To which of the sets *P, R, S, T* do these numbers belong:

(*a*) 1; (*b*) 5; (*c*) 6; (*d*) 9; (*e*) 17; (*f*) 21; (*g*) 36?

2 (*a*) Write down the members of *P, R, S* and *T*.

  (*b*) What can you say about:

   (i) $P \cap R$; (ii) $P \cap S$; (iii) $P \cap T$; (iv) $R \cap S$?

  (*c*) How many members have:

   (i) *P*;   (ii) *T*;   (iii) $P \cap T$?

3 In this question the letters *P, R, S* and *T* stand for the sets:

P = {prime numbers less than 100},
R = {rectangle numbers less than 100},
S = {square numbers less than 100},
T = {triangle numbers less than 100}.

List the members of:

(*a*) $S \cap R$; (*b*) $S \cap T$; (*c*) $P \cap T$; (*d*) $R \cap T$.

(It will help if you write out the members of *T* first.)

4 Copy and complete the following table:

Triangle numbers	Difference	Sum
1st and 2nd	2	4
2nd and 3rd	3	
3rd and 4th		
6th and 7th		
10th and 11th		

Can you find a connection between the 2nd and 3rd columns?

5 Cube Numbers. How many cube blocks of side 1 cm can be fitted into a cubical box whose inner edges are all of length:

(*a*) 1 cm;   (*b*) 2 cm;   (*c*) 3 cm?

The answers are all members of the set of cube numbers. Can you find three more such numbers to add to the set? (Remember that we write 2 cubed as 2^3.)

6 Pyramid Numbers. A pyramid can be made by placing 9 tennis balls in a square, then adding another layer with 4 balls and a top layer of 1 ball. How many balls are needed altogether?

The answer to this is a member of the set of pyramid numbers. Add three more pyramid numbers to those given:

1, 5, 14, ...

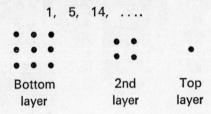

Bottom   2nd   Top
layer   layer   layer

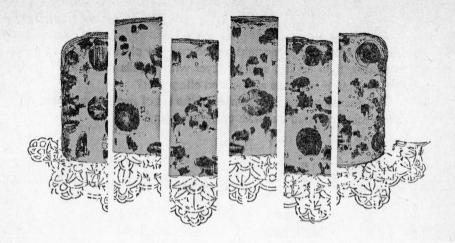

9. Two ways of looking at division

1. REPEATED SUBTRACTION

(*a*) Some people are queueing up for sandwiches, each made from two slices of bread. There are 20 slices, how many are left after:

> 1 person has taken a sandwich;
>
> 2 people have taken a sandwich each;
>
> 3 people have taken a sandwich each?

This is a process of 'repeated subtraction'. It can be continued until there is either one or no slice left. How many people can get a sandwich if there were 17 slices to start with? How many people if there were 117 slices to start with; or 1117?

All those subtractions would have wasted time so you probably used division. In this case division is a quick way of carrying out repeated subtraction, (see Chapter 4, Section 1.2). (For some computers, repeated subtraction is the only way of carrying out division.)

What is left can be stated either as 1 slice, or, as a sandwich is made from 2 slices, as a $\frac{1}{2}$ sandwich.

(*b*) Draw some diagrams to show how 20 bars of chocolate can be arranged in stacks having: (i) 3 bars in each, (ii) 4 bars in each, (iii) 7 bars in each. How many stacks are there in each case? What fraction of a stack is left over?

(*c*) Some children are counting a great pile of tenpenny pieces.

They are doing it by arranging them in 'pound' heaps. Is this repeated subtraction? If you thought that there were 1041 tenpenny pieces altogether, how many heaps would you expect? What fraction of a heap is left?

(*d*) Some extra people joined the queue for sandwiches when there were 117 slices. It was decided to serve $\frac{1}{2}$ sandwiches. How many half sandwiches were available?

117 halves can be written $\frac{117}{2}$ or, from Chapter 6, as $58\frac{1}{2}$. But, in (*a*), we did the division $117 \div 2$ to obtain the answer $58\frac{1}{2}$.

As $\frac{117}{2}$ is a way of writing the answer to $117 \div 2$, it has become a shorthand for division and, for example, $\frac{13}{2}$ may be read '13 divided by 2'.

2. FAIR SHARES

A mother has a family of four children who always insist on their 'fair' share of food! One day she sends them to a nearby shop with Order I. Instead they bring back the things in Order II.

Order I	*Order II*
1 large cream cake	1 large cream cake
2 scones	2 scones
4 doughnuts	3 doughnuts
4 currant buns	5 currant buns
4 tomato sandwiches	4 sandwiches (1 each of cheese, ham, tomato and beef)

Her original order would have been quite easy to divide equally among the four children. How would you have done this? The second order is not so easy, but the mother managed to do it by cutting carefully like this:

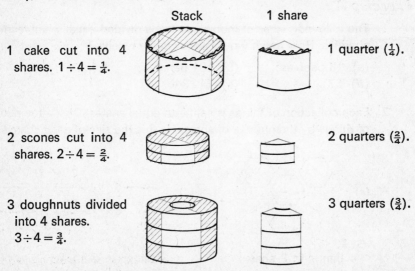

Stack   1 share

1 cake cut into 4 shares. $1 \div 4 = \frac{1}{4}$.   1 quarter ($\frac{1}{4}$).

2 scones cut into 4 shares. $2 \div 4 = \frac{2}{4}$.   2 quarters ($\frac{2}{4}$).

3 doughnuts divided into 4 shares. $3 \div 4 = \frac{3}{4}$.   3 quarters ($\frac{3}{4}$).

Division

4 sandwiches divided
into 4 shares.
$4 \div 4 = \frac{4}{4}.$

| HAM |
| CHEESE |
| TOMATO |
| BEEF |

4 quarters ($\frac{4}{4}$).
(Notice how
'fair' the
mother was
here.)

5 currant buns
divided into 4 shares.
$5 \div 4 = \frac{5}{4}.$

5 quarters ($\frac{5}{4}$).

Whatever number of cakes or sandwiches the mother had, she could always obtain 4 fair shares by this method. Any number can be divided by 4.

Suppose, however, that there had been six children, not four. Draw a picture to show how she would have divided the four sandwiches into 6 equal shares.

To find the number of sweets that each would get if there were 30 altogether, you would again do a division 'sum'. This time we are using division as a method for finding the answer when splitting some collection of objects into equal groups. It is the opposite of multiplication which gives the answer when groups of the same sizes are joined together.

Is it possible to divide by *any* number? If not, what is the exceptional number?

Exercise A

1   The following sums of money are to be divided equally between two charities. How much would each charity receive?

(a) 13 pennies;   (b) 101 pennies;   (c) £48;

(d) £7;   (e) £12345.

2   Each collection of things is split into equal shares. Divide the number of things by the number of shares. Is this the size of each share?

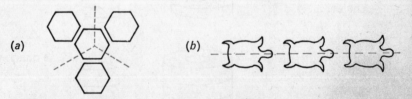

(a)   (b)

4 things in 3 shares   3 things in 2 shares

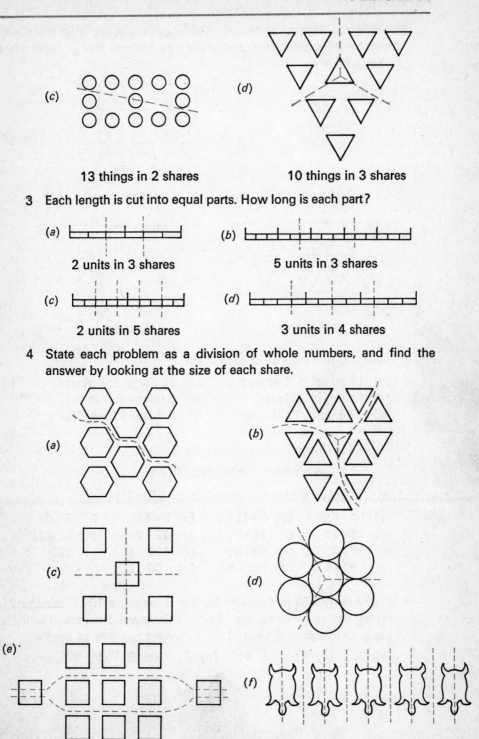

(c)

(d)

13 things in 2 shares   10 things in 3 shares

3 Each length is cut into equal parts. How long is each part?

(a)

2 units in 3 shares

(b)

5 units in 3 shares

(c)

2 units in 5 shares

(d)

3 units in 4 shares

4 State each problem as a division of whole numbers, and find the answer by looking at the size of each share.

(a)

(b)

(c)

(d)

(e)

(f)

Division

5 Trace each group of things. Divide each diagram into the stated number of equal shares, and shade one of these shares. How many things have you shaded?

(a)

2 shares

(b)

4 shares

(c)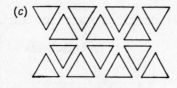

4 shares

(d)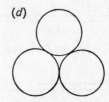

6 shares

6 Divide to find the size of each share:
   (a) 14 things in 2 shares;   (b) 15 things in 4 shares;
   (c) 1 thing in 2 shares;   (d) 6 things in 6 shares;
   (e) 6 things in 12 shares;   (f) 6 things in one share.

7 Give each division as a fraction (e.g. $5 \div 9 = \frac{5}{9}$),

as a whole number (e.g. $18 \div 9 = 2$),

or,   as a mixed number (e.g. $23 \div 9 = 2\frac{5}{9}$).

   (a) $10 \div 5$;   (b) $5 \div 10$;   (c) $5 \div 5$;   (d) $7 \div 5$;
   (e) $18 \div 7$;   (f) $21 \div 7$;   (g) $22 \div 7$;   (h) $72 \div 2$;
   (i) $50 \div 7$;   (j) $50 \div 4$;   (k) $100 \div 3$;   (l) $100 \div 4$;
   (m) $100 \div 5$;   (n) $100 \div 6$;   (o) $100 \div 7$.

8 A Chadbury's 50 g chocolate bar has 8 pieces, a 100 g bar has 21 pieces, and an Airlite bar has 10 pieces. State which bar could be most easily shared among each of the following numbers of people:

   (a) 3;   (b) 4;   (c) 5;   (d) 7;   (e) 2;   (f) 16.

10. Polyhedra

1. NETS

To make a hollow cube, Figure 1, six equal squares are needed. We could cut out all six and then join them with adhesive tape but, as you can see from any cardboard box, this is not necessary. We could draw six equal squares on paper as in Figure 2, cut round the outside and then *fold* them up into a cube.

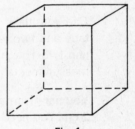

Fig. 1

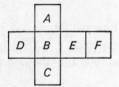 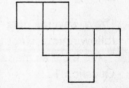

Fig. 2

Six squares can be joined edge to edge in several ways. Figure 2 shows three examples. In the first example, squares *A*, *D*, *E*, *C* could be folded up to form the side faces of a cube with *B* the bottom face and *F* the top face.

(*a*) Can either of the other shapes be folded to form a cube? If you are not sure, copy these shapes on to squared paper. Then cut them out and fold them.

(*b*) On squared paper, draw as many other shapes as you can, made with six squares in this way. Try to decide which of them could be folded to form a cube. Check your results by cutting and folding. How many shapes can you find? Has your neighbour found any shapes which are different from yours?

(*c*) Each of the shapes which can be folded to form a cube is called a *net* of the cube. Which of your shapes are *obviously* not nets of the cube? Why?

Solid figures which have plane faces are called *polyhedra* which means 'having many faces'. (Singular—polyhedron.) In this section, we shall not make the solid figures but only their surfaces.

Exercise A

1 Draw as many shapes as you can by joining five equal squares edge to edge.

Mark those which could be folded to form the bottom and sides of a cubical box without a lid. Exchange books with a neighbour. Do you agree with your neighbour's results?

2 Can you make a rectangular box (or 'cuboid'), using some adhesive tape and two rectangular cards 16 cm by 8 cm, two 8 cm by 6 cm, and two 16 cm by 6 cm? If so, sketch a net for the box. Show the measurements of the cards on your sketch.

3 You are given two rectangular cards 6 cm by 3 cm and two 6 cm by 2 cm. You need two more cards to make a cuboid. What is the size of the missing cards? Draw an accurate net for the cuboid on squared paper.

4 Draw several nets for a rectangular box without a lid given the following measurements: 3 cm long, 2 cm wide and 1 cm high.

Are there as many possible nets as you found for the cubical box in Question 1?

D 5 Cubes, cuboids and the other figures in Figure 3 are all examples of a special type of polyhedron called a *prism*. They all have two ends (those marked in the figure) which are parallel and which are the same shape and size. The faces joining the ends must be parallelograms.

Examples of prisms are an unsharpened pencil (see Figure 3), a ruler, a fiftypenny piece.

Give some more examples. Is a cube a prism?

The ends of the unsharpened pencil in Figure 3 are regular polygons. Name them.

D 6 A prism with circular ends is called a *cylinder*. Are these cylinders: a broom handle, a cocoa tin, a penny?

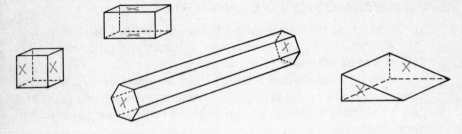

Fig. 3

7 Sketch first the net for a hexagonal prism and then the net for a cylinder. Would you have to make the ends as separate pieces?

8 Figure 4 shows a pyramid with a square base. The four triangular faces have the same shape and size and are isosceles triangles.

(*a*) Sketch a net for this pyramid.

(*b*) Suppose you wanted to construct the pyramid in Figure 4 without the base. Would it be possible to use a similar net now? If not, what different shape of net could you use? (*Hint*: draw a circle.)

(*c*) Would it be possible to include the base in the new shape of net, if you wanted it after all?

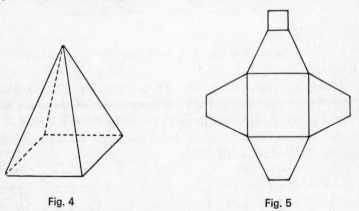

Fig. 4   Fig. 5

9 Figure 5 shows the net of a polyhedron. *Either* describe the polyhedron *or* copy the net and make the polyhedron.

10 Make an accurate model of a triangular prism, the triangular ends being equilateral.

Could you make a hexagonal prism out of a number of these triangular prisms? How many would you need?

2. CONSTRUCTION TECHNIQUES

You will find the following advice helpful when making polyhedra.

1 Accuracy in making a net is very important if a satisfactory polyhedron is to be obtained.

2 Although squares and rectangles can be drawn using ruler, compasses and protractor (or set-square), it is best to use squared paper and prick through the corners of the net on to the material being used for the model itself.

3 Triangles are best constructed with compasses.

4 (a) The flower pattern (see Figure 6) is really a network of equilateral triangles and is useful for making nets of polyhedra with equilateral triangular faces.

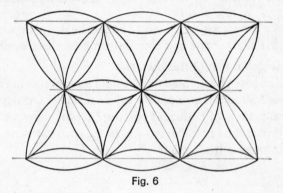

Fig. 6

(b) A pattern of equilateral triangles can also be made by paper folding.

Fold a *large* rectangular piece of paper in half lengthwise, and open out again (see Figure 7 (a)). Fold a bottom corner, B, on to the first fold so that the new fold passes through the other bottom corner A. Turn the paper over and fold AL on to AP. Now open out the paper again (see Figure 7 (d)). Fold along BC.

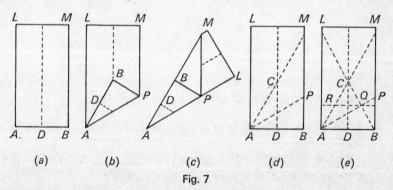

(a)   (b)   (c)   (d)   (e)

Fig. 7

Triangle *ABC* is equilateral.

To continue the pattern, fold triangle *ABC* so that *D* falls on *C* and open out again (see Figure 7 (*e*)). Now fold *A* onto *Q* and *B* onto *R*.

(*c*) The easiest way of obtaining equilateral triangles is to prick through isometric graph paper (see Figure 8). Before using this method you should be sure that you can use successfully at least one of the other two methods.

Fig. 8. Isometric graph paper

5   Coloured card or heavyweight cartridge paper are the best materials for making models. Before folding, run a compass point or other sharp instrument along the lines to be folded; in this way, a clean fold is obtained. Edges may be joined with adhesive tape, but, for a more professional result, use tabs on the edges and stick with a quick-drying glue. If you cannot decide where to put the tabs, put them on all free edges and cut them off when not needed.

Important. Keep one face free of tabs and secure that one last.

3. DELTAHEDRA

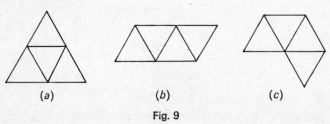

Fig. 9

(*a*)   Figure 9 shows the ways in which four equilateral triangles can be joined edge to edge. Which of these shapes form the net of a pyramid with four equilateral triangular faces (including the base)? Check your answer by cutting these shapes from isometric graph paper and folding them.

A pyramid with four faces all triangular is called a *tetrahedron*. If the triangles are equilateral, it is called a *regular* tetrahedron. A regular tetrahedron looks the same no matter on which face you place it.

(*b*) Name another polyhedron which looks the same no matter on which face you place it.

Polyhedra with equilateral triangular faces are called *deltahedra*. A regular tetrahedron is one example of a deltahedron.

(*c*) (i) Make two equal square-based pyramids, each with four equilateral triangular faces.

    (ii) Stick the square bases together.

    (iii) How many faces has your new polyhedron?

    (iv) Is it a deltahedron?

    (v) Does it look the same no matter on which face you place it?

    (vi) Sketch a net for this new polyhedron.

Your polyhedron has a special name. It is called a regular *octahedron* (see Figure 18).

(*d*) If, for every pair of points of a polyhedron, the line segment joining them lies entirely within the polyhedron, then the polyhedron is said to be *convex*.

Are the following polyhedra convex:

    (i) a cube;

    (ii) a regular tetrahedron;

    (iii) a regular octahedron?

Exercise B

1   Figure 10 shows a net of a regular tetrahedron.

Fig. 10

(*a*) Make two regular tetrahedra.

(*b*) Stick your tetrahedra together to form a deltahedron with six faces.

(*c*) Sketch a net of this new deltahedron. Your net should contain only six equilateral triangles.

2   Draw as many shapes as you can formed by eight equilateral triangles joined edge to edge. Figure 11 shows two examples. How many of the shapes which you have drawn are nets for an octahedron? Only one of those in Figure 11 is such a net. Which one?

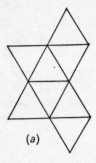
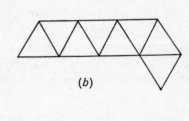

(a)

(b)

Fig. 11

3   Sketch a net for a ten-faced deltahedron formed by two pyramids with pentagonal bases, joined base to base.

4   One important deltahedron is the icosahedron, which has twenty faces. Figure 12 shows one possible net. Use this net to construct an icosahedron.

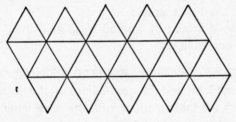

Fig. 12

5   Can a deltahedron have six faces meeting at a vertex? If you think so, make one. If you do not think so, give your reason.

You will need pipe cleaners cut into four pieces and drinking straws cut into two equal parts for Questions 6–8. (Figure 13 shows a neat way of joining three straws.)

6   All the deltahedra we have made so far are convex. Use straws and pipe cleaners to make skeleton models of some deltahedra which are not convex. For example, one can be formed by taking a tetrahedron and sticking an equal tetrahedron on to each of its four faces.

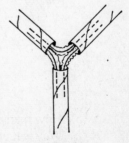

Fig. 13

133

7 You have already made convex deltahedra with four, six, eight, ten and twenty faces. There are three more with twelve, fourteen and sixteen faces respectively. Make skeleton models of these three deltahedra. If you have difficulty, first make the models from card using the nets in Figure 14.

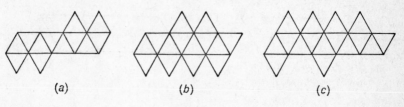

(a)   (b)   (c)

Fig. 14

8 You have now made several skeleton deltahedra. The shape of the triangular faces cannot be changed without bending the straws. Make a skeleton cube. Can the shape of the square faces be easily changed? Which of your models are rigid?

9 Take an octahedron and stick a tetrahedron on to each face. You will get a 'stellated octahedron'.

What solid would be formed by joining the 8 outer vertices of a stellated octahedron?

10 Figure 15 shows a net for a ring of 10 regular tetrahedra. Score the full lines on the front and the dotted lines on the back. Fold the net carefully. Stick the tabs to edges with the same letter (that is, stick tab a to edge a, and so on). The ring can be turned round and round and is therefore called a rotatable ring of tetrahedra.

You can make a ring with more tetrahedra by using a longer net.

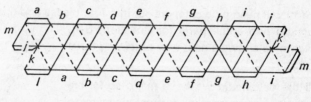

Fig. 15

11 (a) How many faces of a polyhedron meet at an edge?
   (b) Why is it impossible to make a deltahedron with exactly 5 faces?
   (c) Is it possible to make a deltahedron with exactly 9 faces?

4. THE DODECAHEDRON

4.1 Convex regular polyhedra

There are only five regular polyhedra that are convex. They are the ones with 4, 6, 8, 12 and 20 faces. The one with 6 faces is the cube.

Those with 4, 8 and 20 faces are regular deltahedra. If you did Questions 1, 2 and 4 of Exercise B, you will have already made them. What are their names?

The fifth regular convex polyhedron has 12 faces and is called a *dodecahedron*. Its faces are regular pentagons. The net for this is best constructed in two halves. Draw a large regular pentagon by first drawing a circle. Draw all the diagonals and you will find a smaller pentagon inside the first one. Draw the diagonals of the smaller pentagon making them long enough to meet the sides of the larger one (see Figure 16).

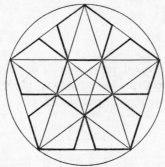

Fig. 16

The thick lines in Figure 16 form half the net of a dodecahedron.

Construct a regular dodecahedron. Do not forget to leave one face free of tabs and secure it last.

4.2 Non-convex regular polyhedra

Two non-convex regular polyhedra are made by adding pyramids to the faces of (a) a dodecahedron, (b) an icosahedron. The nets of the pyramids are shown in Figure 17. You should find out for yourself how many pyramids are needed in each case and also the correct size to make them. The resulting polyhedra are usually called (a) a small stellated dodecahedron; (b) a great stellated dodecahedron.

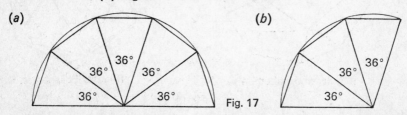

(a)   (b)   Fig. 17

Exercise C

Class projects

1 Make (*a*) a small stellated dodecahedron; (*b*) a great stellated dodecahedron. Why do you think they are called dodecahedra?

2 Make a list of all the polyhedra you have made. Count the number of faces, vertices and edges for each polyhedron. Enter your result in a table, like the following.

Description of polyhedron	Number of faces (F)	Number of vertices (V)	Number of edges (E)
Cube	6	8	12
Octahedron	8		

Look for patterns in your table and comment on those that you find.

SUMMARY

A polyhedron is convex if, for every pair of points of the polyhedron, the line segment joining them lies entirely within the polyhedron.

There are 5 convex regular polyhedra.

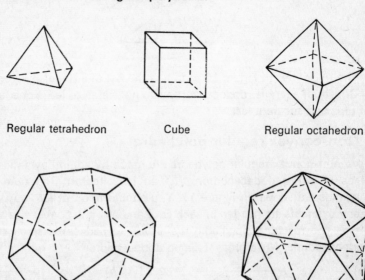

Regular tetrahedron   Cube   Regular octahedron

Regular dodecahedron   Regular icosahedron

Fig. 18

A pyramid is identified by referring to the shape of its base. Figure 19 (*a*) shows a hexagonal pyramid.

A prism is identified by referring to the shape of its 'ends'. Figure 19 (*b*) shows a triangular prism.

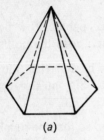

(*a*)

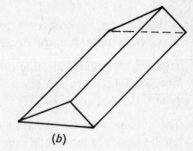

(*b*)

Fig. 19

Puzzle corner

1 A bottle and its cork cost together six pence. The bottle costs five pence more than the cork. How much does the bottle cost?

2 How many squares are there on a chess board? (No, the answer is not just 64! There are squares of eight different sizes on a chess board. How many of each?)

3 The dots on a die are traditionally arranged so that the number of dots on the opposite faces total seven. Keeping the 1 and 6 fixed, in how many ways can the 2 and 5 and 3 and 4 be arranged round them?

4 A frog is at the bottom of a 10 m well. Each hour he climbs up 1 m and then slips back 0·5 m. How many hours does it take him to get out?

5 A park gardener took a great pride in his flower beds. In particular, he liked to put the plants in straight lines. Imagine his delight when one day he discovered that he had planted 9 geraniums so that there were 10 lines with 3 plants in each. Make a drawing to show how 9 geraniums can be planted with just 3 plants in each line making (a) 8 lines (see Prelude), (b) 9 lines, (c) 10 lines.

6 What comes next?
   (a) 5, 7, 11, 19, ...;   (c) 0, 1, 1, 2, 3, 5, ...;
   (b) 2, 6, 12, 20, ...;   (d) 2, 3, 5, 7, 11, ...

7 A boy cycles 3 km to his school each morning. He leaves home at a time which allows him to average 15 km/h and arrive for roll call. One morning the traffic was heavy and he only managed to average 10 km/h for the first two kilometres. What speed must he average for the last kilometre to be in time for roll call?

8 A clock strikes six in 5 seconds. How long does it take to strike twelve?

9 In the following addition each letter stands for a number. What are the other numbers given that E stands for 1 and U stands for 9?

$$
\begin{array}{r}
\mathrm{THREE} \\
\mathrm{THREE} \\
\mathrm{FOUR} \\
\hline
\mathrm{ELEVEN}
\end{array}
$$

10 It is known that a faulty billiard ball has been mixed up with 26 good balls. The balls all look alike but the faulty one is heavier than the others. How can the faulty ball be detected by weighing balls against one another on a pair of scales? What is the smallest number of weighings required?

11 Mark 4 points on paper so that there are only 2 different distances between them. One arrangement is shown in Figure 1.

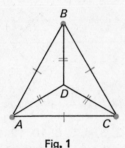

$$AB = BC = CA,$$
$$DA = DB = DC.$$

Fig. 1

There are 6 different possible arrangements. Find two others.

12 A civil engineer had to design a road system connecting 3 towns A, B and C (see Figure 2).

$$AB = 5 \text{ km,}$$
$$BC = 7 \text{ km,}$$
$$CA = 6 \text{ km.}$$

Fig. 2

Naturally the county council wanted to keep the roads as short as possible to reduce the cost. Draw accurate maps of the towns and, by trial and error, find as short a road system as you can. State its length.

Revision exercises

Quick quiz, no. 3

1 Which of these figures are *regular* polygons?

      (a)   (b)   (c)   (d)

2 $\frac{1}{9} + \frac{2}{9} + \frac{4}{9} = ?$

3 If $A = \{$factors of 60$\} = \{1, 2, 3, 4, 5, 6, 10, 12, 15, 20, 30, 60\}$ and $B = \{$*prime* factors of 60$\}$, what are the members of B?

4 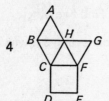 This is a net for a polyhedron. When it is 'made up', what points will be brought to E?

5 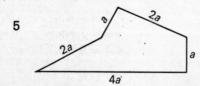 What is the total length of the sides of the figure? (Make your answer as simple as possible.)

6 A line of length 4 cm is divided into 5 equal parts. What is the length of 1 part?

Quick quiz, no. 4

1 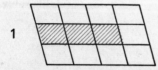 What fraction of this figure is shaded?

2 How many diagonals could be drawn from any one vertex of a 24-sided convex polygon?

3 10 is the fourth triangle number. What is the sixth triangle number?

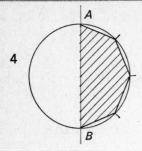

4 *AB* is a line of symmetry of a regular polygon, part of which is shown. How many lines of symmetry has the completed figure?

5 17 identical glasses are filled from 3 bottles of cider. Each bottle contains seven of these glassfuls. What fraction of a bottle of cider remains?

6 $1048 \div 8 = (1000 \div 8) + (48 \div 8)$. True or false?

Exercise C

1 Trace each figure. Put in any lines of symmetry.
  What rotational symmetry does it have about the marked point?

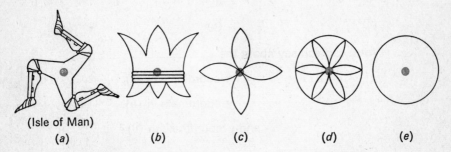

(Isle of Man)
  (a)   (b)   (c)   (d)   (e)

2 Which of the following statements are true and which are false?

(*a*) No prime number is even;
(*b*) the square of an odd number is always an odd number;
(*c*) two square numbers added together never make another square number;
(*d*) two prime numbers multiplied together sometimes make another prime number;
(*e*) apart from 1, no triangle number is also a square number.

3 Draw an eight-sided figure with:

1 line of symmetry,
4 right angles,
3 adjacent sides equal and the other 5 equal to one another.

Is your figure convex? If not, do you think it possible to draw a figure with these properties that is convex?

141

Revision exercises

4 If 3 *P* = {factors of 54},

| *Q* = {prime factors of 42},

3 *R* = {multiples of 3 that are less than 30},

list the members of the sets *P*, *Q* and *R*.
List the members of the sets:

(*a*) *P*∩*Q*;   (*b*) *P*∩*R*;   (*c*) *P*∩*Q*∩*R*.

5   /   2   /

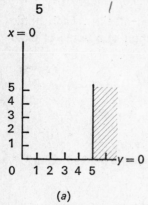

(*a*)

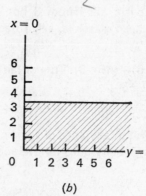

(*b*)

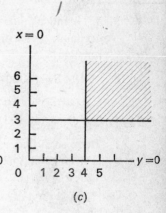

(*c*)

What can you say about the

x-coordinate in (*a*), 2

y-coordinate in (*b*), 2

x- and *y*-coordinate in (*c*)? 4

Exercise D

1 Using squared paper, draw accurately the net for the prism shown:

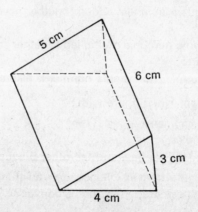

142

2 (*a*) Write down two pairs of prime numbers whose sum is 16.

(*b*) Write down two prime numbers whose difference is 1.

(*c*) Write down two prime numbers whose sum is an odd number.

(*d*) Factorize 48 into primes.

3 Copy and complete the following table. (Note that we are to count only distinct patterns; the two dot patterns shown are considered to be the same.)

Number	18	24	25	30	36	40	49	60	64
Number (*p*) of distinct rectangular patterns	2								
Number (*f*) of factors (excluding 1 and the number itself)	4								

Can you find a connection between '*p*' and '*f*' for:

(*a*) rectangle numbers (excluding square numbers);

(*b*) odd square numbers;

(*c*) even square numbers?

4 Identify the following polygons:

(*a*) 4 lines of symmetry, 4 sides;

(*b*) no lines of symmetry, but rotational symmetry of order 2 and 4 sides;

(*c*) 3 sides and 3 lines of symmetry;

(*d*) 6 lines of symmetry and 6 sides;

(*e*) 8 sides and rotational symmetry of order 8.

5 Which of the following are examples of division as repeated subtraction and which are examples of division as a splitting into equal parts? Write down the numerical answer to each question.

(*a*) How many people can be given exactly 3 fish fingers out of a packet of 16?

(*b*) How many oranges would each person get if a box of 48 was divided between four people?

(*c*) How many sandwiches can be made from a cut loaf of 22 slices?

(*d*) Some cardboard boxes are made to take 60 tins. How many boxes are required if 700 tins are to be packed?

(*e*) 100 litres of water has to be divided between 8 people. How much should each person get?

Revision exercises

Exercise E

1 Copy and complete the patterns shown in the figure. The dotted lines are lines of symmetry, and the red dots are centres of rotational symmetry.

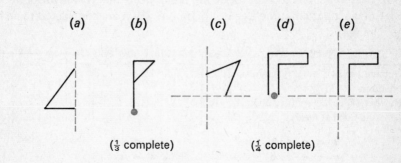

(a)　　　(b)　　　(c)　　　(d)　　　(e)

($\frac{1}{3}$ complete)　　　　　($\frac{1}{4}$ complete)

2 If $A = $ {prime factors of 60},

$B = $ {factors of 20 (excluding 1 and 20)},

$C = $ {square numbers less than 75},

write down the members of each set.
What are: (a) $A \cap B$; (b) $A \cap C$?

3 A man on holiday in Switzerland buys 6 bread rolls at 30 cents each and 3 apple tarts at 50 cents each. How much change does he get from a 5 franc note if there are 100 cents in 1 franc?

4 If the earth revolves about its axis once every 24 hours, through what angle (in degrees) does it turn

(a) in 6 hours;　　　(b) in 1 hour;

(c) in 4 minutes;　　(d) in 2 days?

How long does it take to turn through 20°?

5 A numeral system uses four digits *, ▽, ?, ⊕ (not necessarily in that order) and

$* ▽ ? ⊕ + ? ▽ * ▽ = ▽ ▽ ? ▽ ▽.$

What do the symbols *, ▽, ?, ⊕, represent? Write down the first twenty numbers in this system.

144

(handwritten annotations in margins:)
2,3,5
2,4,5,10
1,4,9,16,25,36,49,64
{2,5} φ
180
150
3.30   1.70
90°
1°   15°   720°
3 0   1 4